THE
THOUGHTS
AND SECRETS
OF SUCCESSFUL
PUNTERS

THE
THOUGHTS
AND SECRETS
OF SUCCESSFUL
PUNTERS

Conversations with Ten Successful Punters
MARK LITTLEWOOD

Published in 2011 by Raceform
Compton, Newbury, Berkshire, RG20 6NL

Copyright © Mark Littlewood 2011

A catalogue record for this book is available from the British Library.

ISBN 978-1-906820-85-5

Designed by Fiona Pike

Printed in Great Britain by the MPG Book Group

CONTENTS

FOREWORD

The vast majority of us started out with a very similar set of influences when we embarked on our betting life. Sadly the habits promoted through these influences become entrenched and as time passes the chance of breaking free becomes ever more difficult. I can remember how these early ideas shaped, or should I say warped, my mind and none can be more fundamentally damaging than the idea that when looking at a race our job is to try to find the winner. Most punters today still think that successful betting is about the next race and finding which horse is most likely to win it. If they fail to make a profit by the end of the year they simply come to the conclusion that their winner-finding technique is not yet sufficiently honed.

All the successful punters I have known understand the important relationship that exists between a bet, the estimated odds of winning, and the actual odds available. To them good bets are not those that won with bad bets simply all the others. Good bets are all those in which odds were obtained which were better than the true chance of the horse. Of course we cannot be always sure that this is the case on an individual basis but at the end of a sufficient sample of bets our bottom line will tell us whether our sample of bets were good bets or not.

Why is it that some punters make this transition to successful betting and others do not? I am convinced through my own personal experiences that the company one keeps offers part of the answer. I can narrow my own positive influences down to around five or six, with one of the most important being the discovery of *SmartSig* or *SmarterSig* as it is now known. Here was a betting community that seemed to be inhabited by people who understood the basic equations of betting. Talking and thinking amongst them had the direct effect of changing my betting which eventually allowed me to help others.

INTRODUCTION

They say that that if you average the wealth of your six closest friends you will know exactly how much you earn or more importantly how much you are likely to earn. The same can be said about betting. The company you keep will invariably dictate the profitability of your betting. This is particularly true when you set out on your punting life. Of course very few of us are lucky enough to be mentored early on by a knowledgeable and successful punter, but it's never too late to listen/read and change.

Mixing with successful punters can be almost as difficult as cutting a profit in the first place. Some by nature are introverted, others simply like to keep a low profile for a variety of reasons. There are, however, solid punters out there willing to talk about their perspective on betting.

This book contains a selection of interviews with successful and proven punters. Over the years they have demonstrated their ability to make consistent profits from backing horses, and by reading their views on betting you are opening up the possibility of replacing your six closest betting friends with a number of successful players, if only for a brief period. One thing for sure, there is a wide diversity of approaches amongst successful punters and amongst the players interviewed in this book.

There are many ways to cut a profit. Some players like Russell Clarke are statistically based while others such as Laurence Lambourn take a more visual and interpretative route. Some players avoid certain race types whilst others welcome them with open arms. It matters little as long as it works for you and it is finding not just a profitable angle but also one that suits you that is the key.

What I can say with certainty is that the earlier you mix with successful punters the quicker and more likely you are to turn into one yourself. Is there any common ground amongst the interviewees in the book?

I can say that they all take a businesslike approach to their betting. As Russell Clarke says, betting for a living has much in common with running any other type of business. They understand the fundamentals of good money management, as all good business people do. They have self belief and self motivation in what is often a solitary occupation and of course an ability to stick with it when things are not going so well.

I hope you enjoy the book and derive some betting value from its content.

I would like to express my gratitude to all those who agreed to be interviewed for the book and to the members of SmarterSig.com who have played such a large part in my own betting progress.

Chapter 1

HUGH TAYLOR

Hugh could be described as the Pricewise of At The Races, tipping value horses via the website at around 10.00am every day. Giving daily tips means his tipping profile quickly builds up and his prowess can be checked via a past results section on the site. Hugh also had a spell as a jockeys' agent before joining ATR.

We met up on a Wednesday evening in his home town at the King's Head pub. Having two pubs of that name almost resulted in us sitting quietly drinking our pints some two miles apart but thankfully an early arrival by me allowed enough time to spot my mistake. A good job too, because a thoroughly enjoyable evening was had. Hugh is a very open and honest kind of guy and hopefully that comes across in these notes.

Q. How did you first get involved in racing and betting?

From the age of about five I was taken racing at various Yorkshire courses by an elderly family friend, who obviously liked a bet. I can remember being asked by him to follow a bearded chap in order to see what he was backing. This turned out to be Phil Bull; I thought he looked like Fagin from *Oliver Twist* but I probably looked like the Artful Dodger myself, trailing him round whilst trying to look innocent. I spent a lot of my childhood Saturdays in the 1970s at the Yorkshire courses, and my interest really picked up again after university when I took a job close to Lingfield racetrack.

Q What other jobs have you been involved in and how did the ATR connection evolve?

After university I worked in a large residential school for children with epilepsy, and was in charge of one of the residential units there for 12 years. The school was close to Lingfield racecourse and I was a regular visitor there on my days off. The draw bias at Lingfield was very strong at the time and this was when I realized that having an edge was the key criterion to successful betting. By my mid-thirties I had decided that I was ready for a career change (residential social work is really a young person's job in my opinion). I had already written one or two articles as a hobby and put in a speculative application when I noticed an advert for content writers for the newly-formed Arena Online. I was slightly surprised to get the job and fortunately Arena Online became significant partners in At The Races version one, and I was given the opportunity to write my own column on the website and make quite a few appearances on the channel.

When At The Races #1 folded, I was lucky enough to be offered the job as agent for Kerrin McEvoy, who had just been appointed as Godolphin's number two UK jockey. The job interview for this post was fairly startling – they flew me out to Dubai and shortly after my interview with Simon Crisford at Al Quoz had started, Sheikh Mohammed unexpectedly walked into Simon's office and proceeded to hold court, which was fascinating. I continued to do occasional freelance work for At The Races #2 and also for the *Racing Post* during the winter, and then when Kerrin returned to Australia to become Darley's number one jockey, I was offered the full-time post as the ATR website's lead tipster.

Q How would you describe your early punting career and your progress through to profitable betting?

It was lucky that Lingfield was my local track, because after recognizing the draw bias there, which was probably underestimated at the time (late 1980s), I found it relatively easy to make money there almost from the start. It's probably true to say that I did not do so well at other tracks but overall I was doing okay. The Lingfield experience taught me that you have to find an angle that is not fully factored into the betting market. I also came to a very early conclusion that I found it easier finding overpriced horses amongst the bigger prices than the shorter ones (which doesn't mean that short-priced horses can't be value too, of course, just that I wasn't so good at finding those types of bets).

Q What were the pivotal influences over the years that transformed your betting?

I would describe it as a gradual process; certain books had a little influence but watching races was and remains the biggest education. The importance of knowing something the market doesn't was quickly at the forefront of my mind. I remember having worked out within a few months of starting betting that having as many accounts as possible and searching for the best prices was common sense, and I remember being a bit disappointed when Mark Coton's Pricewise feature started in the *Racing Post*, as I was already in the habit of sifting through the adverts on Teletext and in the *Post/Life* to work out which bookmakers I would be ringing up and obviously it made it that bit harder to get the early prices; I'm fully aware that nowadays people sometimes end up cursing me for the same reasons. Price is everything in betting.

Q Do you think the media helps or hinders the punter? Who would you recommend reading or listening to?

The racing media gets plenty of criticism, and a lot of it is deserved, but there are some very good people too. I'm impressed by people like Richard Hoiles and John Hunt who are not only high-class commentators but also excellent presenters/interviewers and clearly have a passion for the game. There are certainly plenty of people on TV who are far more charismatic in front of a camera than I am, that's for sure. In terms of books, I think Alan Potts' two publications were both full of sense, and some of the American authors can be helpful if you can adapt their thinking to British racing. A lot of people seem to regard *Timeform* as outdated these days but personally I still find them a very useful tool.

Q Your ATR tipping page has developed quite a following. Are there any development plans for this?

The website editor Matthew Taylor, who has been tremendously supportive towards me, initially wanted me to provide tips overnight or at least by 9.00am to enable as many people as possible to read them before work etc, but within a very short period of time the impact of the selections on the market meant we had to wait until around 10.00am to enable readers to at least have a range of early prices to have a crack at; Matthew is very realistic and fully agreed with this. However, we are fully aware that readers have major problems getting on at the price advised and there is little sign of any bookmaker offering to guarantee prices to any degree whatsoever.

We have had a few discussions about how to improve the service and these are ongoing. One thing I would say is that since day one I have tried to make the column more than just a series of tips; the reasoning behind every selection has always been given and I have tried to provide as wide a variety of angles as possible, as not every punter is interested in being spoon-fed tips. When I listen to people talking about their bets, it's how they reach their selections that I find more interesting than the selections themselves.

Q Do you manage to get on with your bets?

It's tough. I have umpteen accounts but a great number of them are now unusable. Unfortunately this is nothing unusual nowadays and having accounts closed (or as tends to happen more often, restricted) is no longer the badge of honour that it was ten or twenty years ago, as any half-successful punter will be aware. There are a handful of firms that will still lay me a respectable bet but I'm never quite sure which of them are just doing it because it's useful to them to know what I'm backing as soon as possible; they will have learned by now that I don't back my selections until they are online anyway. It does make me laugh when people suggest that I back my selections before they go online to arb them back. I've never arbed any of my selections, and if I was backing them before they went online, you'd soon know, because the prices would be gone. Anyone who keeps a close eye on the column will be able to tell you that the prices do go very fast – often in seconds – but they go after the column is online, not before; we have three different guys who upload the column and I can guarantee they don't back them before it goes online, either.

Q Is there any danger that the last nine months represent an over-performance on your part?

It's hard to answer this because it's the first time I have been paid to give my full attention to full-time tipping. I think it's a case of so far, so good given that every month since I started in March has been profitable to advised stakes (and I take on board the problems of getting on), though realistically that can't go on forever – I can promise you I've had plenty of losing months over my betting lifetime – and long losing runs are inevitable for punters/tipsters going for bigger-priced horses.

Q From a betting point of view do you prefer Flat, AW, chases, hurdles?

I love National Hunt racing as a spectacle but from a betting point of view I feel I have more angles relating to the Flat, probably because that's where my attention has been focused over the last five years.

Q Describe a typical day from a betting/race analysis point of view.

By 8.00am I am in my office starting to finalize my selections although I will have done the groundwork, often pricing up a selection of races, the previous day. I do think it's important to assess a race before you have seen any betting forecasts; I think it's very hard to be objective about value when you are aware of likely prices before you start to look at the form. If I am appearing on TV then I usually pre-write the column the night before with a variety of possible selections and then narrow it down when prices start to become apparent in the morning, as I have to leave relatively early to get to the studios in London from my home in Guildford and time is very tight – I usually have a variety of horses on the day that I think might be overpriced. Of course, there are occasions when the price I envisaged does not materialize and then the column needs a quick rewrite. Once the column and selections have been forwarded I begin the process of looking at the next day. I am really lucky to be doing something for a living that I genuinely enjoy. It's not really about the money or the winnings but the kick of finding those overpriced horses.

Q Is there a particular starting point that shapes your approach to analyzing a race?
It's usually the tape first. I have a DVD recorder with a 400GB hard drive that can hold most of a Flat season. I record every Flat meeting (and an increasing number of NH ones) and try to watch every race, looking for horses that have run better than their bare form suggests. I use one of the many email horse alert services that are available nowadays to help me keep track of my notes – I have well over 200 noted horses at present – and these often form the starting point of my analysis. I couple this with angles that, in my opinion, the market might be underestimating such as pace, track bias or a particular trainer's performance with a category of horse. In a ten-runner race I would probably scrutinize the past video performance of maybe eight of the runners, and then price them up.

Q Do you keep negative notes or alerts of horses to oppose?
No, not really, obviously finding a bad favourite can help with finding value in the same race but I'd rather concentrate on the horses that I think are likely to be overpriced.

Q Any advice on coping with the inevitable losing run?
It is the hardest thing to handle with betting and probably the single reason why most punters shy away from bigger-priced runners. Most big-priced runners are actually underpriced in relative terms compared to market leaders – for instance, 33-1 shots have only won 1.6% of their races in Britain since 2000, which means the average

33-1 shot is nearer a 66-1 shot. This makes finding the overpriced ones even harder but you simply have to take the long-term view, and not all 33-1 shots are the same!

Q What form do your actual bets take; straight win, each-way, exotic, in-running, trading?
I generally find that win only is more profitable for me although I do some EW where it's advantageous, for example 16+ runner handicaps. I generally don't get involved with in-running betting simply because I'm not good enough at it, the emphasis on making swift decisions doesn't suit me.

Q Are you obliged to tip every day?
Yes, I am contracted to supply a tipping column every day (holidays excepted, obviously).

Q Have Rule 4s been applied to your website bet history?
Yes, I try to be quite careful about that side of things though it can be difficult to be precise when a selection was advised at a price offered by several different firms. I even take care not to register prices that might have disappeared between me posting the column and its first show on the website. To be honest I only originally kept records for my own information as I don't think anybody involved with the website quite expected the level of interest the column has attracted; we only started publishing the records because we got lots of requests to do so.

Q What are the betting tools that you utilize to analyze a race?
Video, *Timeform* and *Raceform Interactive*. I'm no technical wizard by any means but I think I know how to get the best out of the tools

I do use. The internet is obviously useful for searching for weather details, trainer comments and of course the horse alerts.

Q Faced with a punter who does not lose too much, wanting to break into long-term profitable betting, what advice would you give?
Find an angle that the market does not take fully into account. Try to think in terms of the market rather than winner-finding, even if that seems an alien concept at first. If form rather than statistics is your main angle, try and watch as many races as you can – there are numerous online race replay services that can allow you to scrutinize past races. You have to come to a race knowing something about a horse or horses that the market is not fully aware of, and it's tough to do that just from reading the form book without making your own interpretations.

Q Going back to the odds line creation process, tell me a little about how you set about this task.
No real secrets here, I'll have a look at each horse in turn in racecard order to get a flavour of the race, then go through them again and try and put a price on them. The first few times you go through this you'll need an odds-to-percentages converter but after a while you should be hitting close to a 100% book without too much difficulty. I'm not convinced you can use ratings as a shortcut to an odds line, though – you have to be able to make a thorough assessment of everything that impacts on a horse's chance. For instance, if you don't have a grasp of which trainers often significantly improve a newly acquired horse, you could end up putting a 3-1 shot in at 20-1, which renders your tissue useless.

Q What role does statistical analysis play in your selection process?

Done correctly, statistical analysis simply provides proof rather than conjecture, and protects us from the limitations of our own experience. In this day and age, there's no excuse for making glib statements about, say, trainers' records in a particular environment based on one's own limited observations when databases can provide the truth of the matter. What I would say is that an understanding of the use of statistics can become much more powerful when married to an understanding of racing and how betting markets work. For instance, it would be a pointless exercise running a search to find out how well horses with the saddlecloth number 6 perform in handicap chases, or how horses with number 11 do in maidens – but the performance of horses wearing number 1 in Flat claimers is a very valid search, yet you wouldn't know to search that out, or why the positive results are relevant, without a knowledge of how claimers work and what motivates trainers to allocate the weight their horse is given.

I'm rather fortunate in that most of the statistical analysis that has previously been used in the mainstream media has been pretty much garbage ("seven of the last ten favourites won this race" etc); most members of *Smartersig* would be far more sophisticated than me in this field but I'd like to think I have a reasonable grasp of what sort of analysis is relevant.

Q How difficult is it to balance the demands of punting and pundit work with the rest of your life?

I am married with two young children, and apart from half an hour to finalize my Sunday selections from the shortlist I reached the previous day, I spend Sundays with the family, with the DVD recorder running of course. The days when I travel into the studio obviously impact on the amount of research and race-watching I can do; the journey is fragmented into a number of short train/tube journeys, none of which allow any meaningful amount of time to get some work done. There are never enough hours in the week, but I can't complain.

Q What are your ambitions in life generally and specifically racing/betting?
I don't think I'm as motivated by money as a lot of people seem to be – it's more important to have a job that I enjoy and it's just as important to me that people find my work interesting. My family is the most important thing to me, and I'm just very lucky that I have a job which I love that allows me to work from home and see plenty of them.

INTERVIEWED IN DECEMBER 2009

Chapter 2

ALAN POTTS

Alan Potts is one of those pro punters who other pros seem to respect. Maybe it's because they cut their own teeth on his books from the 1990s or maybe it's simply because he is a genuinely helpful kind of guy who doesn't mind giving other punters advice. His early book *Against the Crowd* had a great influence on my thinking and I was happy when he agreed to an interview.

Q How did you first get interested in horseracing and betting?

Betting was always something I enjoyed from an early age – pontoon with my uncles, sixpence each-way on the National, checking my dad's football pools, all from the age of six or seven onwards. The legalization of betting shops came when I was 14, so the timing was perfect for a teenager that liked to bet. I was a maths whizz at school and that side of betting and racing was part of the appeal.

I saw my first horse race live when I was playing cricket one Monday evening on a ground in the centre of the loop at Alexandra Palace near my home in North London – the horses effectively raced round the boundary and it looked a lot more exciting than cricket. I went back a week later and that was my first race meeting – I was aged 14.

Within two years I was working in the local betting shop on Saturdays and during the school holidays.

Q How successful or unsuccessful were you when you first started to bet regularly, did you serve the typical losing apprenticeship?

I went through all the usual phases of form book, systems, tipsters and pins. Losing was certainly my normal experience through the 60s and 70s. Like all punters I remember the winners, but only once did I win enough to actually justify all the effort. The autumn of 1976 was very wet after a drought and I had a golden two months backing soft-ground performers who had no form because the ground had been rock hard all summer. The winnings helped to pay for new furniture and a car (a Triumph TR6, one of my lifelong ambitions).

I'd say it took me twenty years to learn how to consistently break even and another five to become a regular winner.

Q Twenty years sounds familiar to me. Looking back do you think there could have been a shorter route to finding a consistently profitable approach?

Given the lack of educational material available in that era and the paucity of information, I can't think of anything that would have made much difference. The internet has changed betting, but it's far more important as a source of information when combined with the ability to use computers to analyze that information. The amount of time that would have been needed to collect information, let alone do the research, simply wasn't practical alongside a full-time job and a reasonable social life. It's indicative of the lack of sophistication of the 70s that I could actually win money (occasionally) just by identifying a small group of horses that relished soft ground.

To give an example, I saw a filly called Lucent hack up in a soft-ground maiden at Doncaster on TV as a two-year-old. The following summer, she turned up in the entries for a handicap at a Windsor evening meeting I was planning to attend. It rained all day before the racing and I backed her with total confidence – but I'd guess at least 90% of punters had no idea that she was better on soft ground, because the only way to know was to have remembered that race from the previous year.

Q Could you cite any pivotal moments or influences in your early regular betting life that shaped your style and approach to successful betting?

The first bet that persuaded me there was a pattern that I could interpret was at my beloved Ally Pally. It was spring 1969, the horse was called Little Earwig – he'd finished second over the course and distance and was a few pounds better off with the winner. I was sure he could reverse the form and had £30 at 100/30 with a course bookie (to put that sum in perspective, I bought a new house later that year and my monthly mortgage payment was £39). He won OK, although I can't remember any other winners from 1969 and I doubt if the £100 lasted very long!

Q How would your summarize your style of betting? I get the impression that you are not a systems man but someone who is confident and relies on his own judgment about what is a good bet.

Inevitably it's changed a lot over the years, but the basics since I stopped being a loser have been to watch a lot, listen a little, ignore 'inside information', be cynical about hype and rely on my own judgment. My ideal was always to go for the big return, so that when I found a decent-priced winner, the profit was substantial and worthwhile.

Q What would be a typical betting day for you?

Not more than two hours early morning with the form book, often a lot less – by watching all the racing, I find I can absorb a lot of information that I don't have to look up again. My current approach, which is almost the total opposite of what I've done most of my life, is to concentrate on short-priced horses, either backing or laying them on Betfair.

So the first task is to identify the races I'm interested in and all the 3/1 the field handicaps get the chop immediately. Then focus on the favorite and establish the positives and negatives for that horse – using form, time, draw, going, stable form, jumping ability etc to set a target price.

Then check prices on Betfair and monitor the markets up to the start of racing. I watch most racing, although I might draw the line at some of the low-grade evening meetings, and I'm constantly looking for horses of interest for next time (positive or negative) and for patterns in the racing that might indicate any form of bias on the track. A typical example of that would be horses running well from a bad draw or vice-versa. I have a method of splitting big-field results by draw to see if any horse stands out – e.g. in a 16-runner race, look at the horses drawn 1 – 8 as if that was a separate race. If one horse from that group beat the other seven by a wide margin, he's almost certainly run better than the bare result of the overall race suggests.

I also reserve up to an hour per day for a review of races and bets and I do a weekly round-up on Sunday or Monday. As a general rule, I don't bet on Monday or Tuesday and keep those days clear as my 'weekend'.

Q **Do you have any particular methods or approaches to handling a bad run of results? Could you give an example of a typical poor run?**
Not difficult to find an example of a losing run as I'm on one at present! I made around £50k in 2004 and 2005, £20k in 2006 and was over £30k up for 2007 at the end of last October. Since then I've had two winning months that produced less than £1k profit between them and the other three months have seen a loss of £20k. At the time of writing, April 2008 is level. So I'm down over £19k for the last six months.

I handle that by sticking to my approach, recognizing that there's nothing very unusual about such a run. My experience over the last 20 years is that profit comes in bursts and that much of the time I'm either treading water or losing slowly. Losing an average of £3k per month over a six-month period is no surprise, although it's the longest such period I've experienced for several years.

I use what I guess a shrink would call positive reinforcement – I go back to times when I won big, watch the videos of those races, read my account books and diaries, all with the intention of reminding myself what is possible. I'll also take a short break from betting to get negative thoughts out of my system – I did that most recently the week after Aintree earlier this month.

Q Does it not worry you that the week after Aintree could have been a superb week for you or do you feel during these periods that your judgment needs a rest and therefore the break is unavoidable?

I'm certain that regular breaks from betting are essential (although perhaps my age is an influence – I turned 60 last August). When I started out full time in 1991, there was no Sunday racing, far fewer evening meetings and generally less racing than there is today. Also since, like almost all professionals then, I bet on course, by only going racing three or four days per week the workload was kept manageable. With the volume of racing we have now, I'm quite sure that keeping mentally fresh is a big help – sit and do this seven days per week, 52 weeks of the year and you'd go stir crazy. Read the Betfair forum any day for evidence!

It's possibly a harsh judgment, but I feel that most losing punters go on losing because they never stop to actually think about what they are doing (and of course the non-stop nature of the 'product' these days is designed to achieve exactly that).

Q My impression of your betting is perhaps one of quality rather than quantity. I believe in the past you have averaged around 300 – 400 bets a year. Is this correct or has it changed?

Fifteen years ago, soon after I turned full time and was doing almost all my betting on course, I had around 300 bets in a year and concentrated on the better racing.

Ten years ago, that was still the same, with the addition of spread betting as an off-course activity that provided useful profits for a short period (a couple of years) until the firms effectively removed my edge.

Five years ago, the high-stake single win bet at 'value' prices was still my staple, but the internet was changing the world, the on-course market was suffering and I could see that I needed to alter my approach.

Now, I've given up the high-stakes single win, mostly because I could no longer find the value, such has been the impact of the exchanges and the limitless supply of information available to punters. I work almost exclusively with short-priced horses on Betfair, because that's where the liquidity is greatest and that's where an edge can still be found. If this losing run continues for a few more months, I'll have to think again!

Betting on course is no longer an option, as away from the big meetings, there isn't the money there any more, the bookies I knew and worked with have mostly retired or sold up and the costs of travel and admission (time as well as money) are now a significant factor. Why spend three hours in my car on the motorway to stand in the cold and wet taking worse prices than I could get in my office at home in the warm and dry?

So I have changed from a high stakes, low turnover punter to a low stakes, high turnover player on the exchanges. To clarify that, by high stakes I mean backing horses to win five to ten thousand, by low stakes I mean laying them to lose £400 to £500. On average I bet around thirty races per week, so I'm turning over more money and accepting a lower percentage return.

Q I can see why you are laying at the shorter end but does this mean you are also backing at the shorter end of the market, using the exchanges to grind out a smaller return but on a higher turnover?

Yes – at a rough estimate, I'm turning over about £750,000 per annum and making around 4% after commission averaged over the last five years. The split of laying to backing would be around 70/30 and the back bets do still include horses outside the short price range, but to much smaller stakes than I would have used on course.

The basic method is to ensure the maximum loss on a race cannot exceed a set limit (currently £500) – the betting on a race might include more than one lay, or a mix of back and lay on different horses.

Q Do you bet on events other than horseracing? How about laying and trading, do they play any significant part in your activities?

I have dabbled with various sports, but never at the same level as my betting on racing. Just occasionally a price will catch my eye – at the start of this football season, I took the 6-4 for Reading to finish in the bottom six and that looks like producing a profit that will help the account for May. But that's the only football bet I've had in the last 12 months – I don't bet on individual matches.

Q What do you see as the key characteristics needed in a successful professional gambler?

Self confidence, belief, arrogance – call it what you will, but if you harbour doubts about your ability to succeed, you will fail.

The ability to take the long-term view – the idea commonly debated on the Betfair forum that you can set a target to win so much per day is frankly laughable. It's one thing to have a target of £x thousand per year and then calculate what that means in daily terms, but to say, I'll win £x today and then stop is plain daft.

The mental strength to deal with the negative view that most of society will take of your chosen profession. There are no estate agents advertising million-pound houses in the Surrey professional punter belt.

Flexibility – what worked then doesn't work now, what works now probably won't work by 2012.

Q What are your tools of the trade so to speak?
What range of facilities and by that I mean visuals,
ratings, books and anything else that contributes to
your daily profession.

Racing Post delivered by the local wholesale depot at 6.00am, *Timeform Perspective* delivered by post. Laptop with the Post website, Betfair and the BHA website (only available as I'm an owner, but useful as the best source of going reports, non-runners, entries and declarations) as the main sites used. Sky via satellite dish for ATR and RUK. Total cost of these things around £2,200 per annum.

All fairly simple and basic – I don't bet in-running, so I've not found any need to use an interface with Betfair. I stick to paper for the Post and Perspective as I spend enough time gazing at a computer screen already. The key piece of equipment is the one inside my skull!

Q There will always be a nucleus of people
contemplating becoming a full time pro in
the betting world. What are the positives and
negatives of such a working lifestyle?

The positives are much as they always were – freedom from routine, the feeling of doing something that is beyond most people, the pleasure of turning a hobby into a living.

The negatives, especially in the modern era – solitude, the hours spent in front of a computer screen and a TV, the difficulty of going back if things don't work out.

Q Finally, if I presented to you a willing wannabe professional who is the type of punter who doesn't lose a lot over the year but cannot quite break into the regular profit zone, what advice would you offer them? Are there any simple tips that might improve the bottom line by the required amount?

Make a plan – what races will you bet on, how many bets, what stakes and so on. You can't start any business without a plan and this one is no different.

Specialize – it's old advice, but it's still valid.

Analyze – especially analyze your losers post-race. Is there a pattern that you can break out of and either stop making so many losing bets, or even turn some of them into winners. It goes without saying that this sort of analysis depends on you having proper records of your bets. When I became a full-time punter, I found after five years that I was backing the same number of winners per annum, but fewer losers – and that was the key difference in my accounts.

INTERVIEWED IN MAY 2008

Chapter 3

LAURENCE LAMBOURN

Laurence is a professional punter and the man behind www.equineinvestments. co.uk, a tipping service that does exactly what it says on the tin. Something you can't say about all tipping services. He has been a longstanding member of *SmarterSig* and offers plenty of helpful advice on the *SmarterSig* email forum.

Q How did you first get interested in horseracing and betting?

It was around the last couple of years of secondary school when I first started betting on horses. One of the sixth formers used to act as a bookie – he even had his own slips printed – I can distinctly remember 'sydbrokes' across the top of the slip. The catalyst I think was when my mother and I moved in with her partner around 1985. Albert used to bet most days in his local betting shop. Although I didn't know what a mug punter was then, on reflection, I now realize that Albert was a typical example and the bad habit was wearing off on me.

Q How successful or unsuccessful were you when you first started to bet regularly, did you serve the typical losing apprenticeship?

I was young and naïve and had no idea what value was and probably didn't care anyway. I would bet most days and lose steadily and regularly.

Q Could you cite any pivotal moments or influences in your early regular betting life that shaped your style and approach to successful betting?

It was around ten years ago when I did some internet research on racing tipsters. I found what I thought was a suitable chap who made a regular profit. He sent me some past results which I was satisfied with and I gave him a go. It turned out to be a great move, not only did he supply me with profitable bets for three or four years but I could ask him all sorts of questions on his selection criteria and got to know most of the positive factors he looked for in a bet. He mostly specialized in two-year-old races. From this point I knew the game could be cracked and I started to read more betting books and soon began to show a small but steady profit from my own selections. The Racing Systems Builder (RSB) database I bought was a very good tool for me to do my own research on positive and negative factors, it was money well spent.

Q How do you use these positive and negative factors, for example do you feed them into some sort of automated mathematical model or do you use them to influence your own view and judgment on a race?

No not an automated system, more the latter really. I like to list next to each horse all the positives and negatives that I have and then use this to get a feel for the shape of a race.

Q Do you then create odds for every horse?

I can do but these days I tend to narrow the race down to X contenders and then allocate Y/1 for all the other runners. From here I can then estimate my true odds for the contenders, with the number of contenders obviously having an influence on the odds I allocate. After this I generally look for +30% over my true odds.

Q Can you give us an example of a positive or a negative?

Yes, one positive would be a race with a sole pace horse. Some of these positives or negatives are not just statistical but are arrived at from hours of note-taking after studying video playbacks of races.

Q Getting back to when you turned pro, how long ago was this and how did it happen?

It was about eight years ago. I was faced with a choice of redundancy or having my job role changed to one which I didn't care for along with a reduction in wages.

Q Was it a tough decision or were you already performing to the level of a pro?

In some ways yes as I had a family to support and, no, I wasn't making the required amounts at the time to live off, but I was making a profit and as I said before I had realized that the game could be cracked. It was probably a year or two too soon to be honest but I decided to go for it.

Q How did the first year go?

I gave my wife a lump sum to cover the basic living costs for the year and set out with a remaining 9k betting bank. After six months the bank was down to 4K so I cannot say that it was a smooth start. By the end of the year the bank was back up to 12K. The 3K profit was only enough to set me out on the first four months of the following year but things did start to pick up and in the second year I made a 14K profit.

Q What were the factors that influenced the progression in the second year?
Probably the positive and negative ingredients that I was beginning to uncover along with a growing appreciation of value betting.

Q Can you give a clearer picture of some of the mistakes you made in your early pro days?
One that springs to mind is being swayed by press hype on horses, also following prices down. You have to have a price in mind and stick to it. If the price has gone then leave it to the 'a winner is a winner' brigade.

Q To the punter who does better than average but can't quite make a profit, what advice would you give?
Get the best price you can and perhaps log the bets down and then review after say three months. Remember it's all about the prices. Perhaps try and come up with prices for your fancies and stick with them. If the prices don't appear then leave the bet. Creating the prices can initially be quite simple. For example divide a race into genuine contenders, those you can't rule out and those you really don't like at all. So for example you may think that four horses are the main ones with two having some sort of chance and the rest you simply don't like at all. To keep things simple you could maybe combine the two into one contender giving five in all. Now you need 4-1 on the contenders to be a fair price and perhaps 11-2 on them for a bet.

Q What camp are you in on the subject of staking?

I would suggest a similar stake on most selections but certainly don't shy away from your usual stake on longer shots.

Q Where do you want to be in say ten years' time?

I love the game so I still see myself betting but I like the idea of trimming down a little. Maybe betting only in the winter months and then having the summer off. There is so much racing in the summer that you can easily lose track of things.

Q How different did you find the contrast between personal betting and tipping customers?

I must admit at first there was some pressure but I gradually became accustomed to it. The losing runs do weigh heavier on your shoulders though. I do know that not everybody can do it. Some very good punters find it difficult to be good tipsters.

Q On the subject of losing runs, any advice on how to handle them?

Look back and find a similar period in your records. Also check how they have run in the recent poor period. You may find that a few photo finishes made the difference between a reasonable month and a poor one. Sometimes I even look at the bets all over again and ask myself, am I still happy with that bet?

INTERVIEWED IN MARCH 2008

Chapter 4

RUSSELL CLARKE

Russell Clarke may be known to some readers from his monthly column in the now defunct magazine *Odds On*. Russell ran a column on the statistical side of betting along with a very successful advisory service. A clue to how well he had done can be gleaned from the fact that some of this interview took place in a restaurant at the Marina in Marbella, after which Russell took me to see the location of his new-build villa overlooking the city. Russell's Betfair profit alone is in excess of seven figures, a fact I can personally verify. This was clearly a guy worth listening to and another major influence on my own betting. Since this interview Russell has come back to the UK where his daughters are finishing their education.

Q How did you first get interested in horseracing and betting?

I was probably around ten years old when I first took an interest in horseracing. Both my grandad and my uncle were keen punters and the house always had a copy of *The Sporting Life* as we all lived together at that time.

My grandad read all of the views of the racing correspondents in the papers at the bookmakers and then came to a conclusion based on that pool of knowledge. My uncle took a more analytical approach by compiling his own speed figures and keeping the records on index cards. As a youngster I often did the simple maths involved and helped him maintain the cards.

I became fascinated by the concept that the winner of a race could actually be worked out by the use of numbers or ratings. From there it was a natural progression to have a small "round robin" (my bet of choice at that age!)

Q How successful or unsuccessful were you when you first started to bet regularly, did you serve the typical losing apprenticeship?

I didn't keep records back then, so I would be guessing, but my stakes were very small and I fondly remember a number of very good wins, so I would guess that my pre-teen betting days were profitable. As I got older, I did bet more regularly, but it was the 70s and I was lucky enough to be using the speed figures from the old *Sporting Chronicle Handicap Book*. These figures were powerful and largely anonymous to the general betting public and so I was fortunate to have stumbled upon a source of profit.

I don't suffer from a need to win on any given day and so have never chased losses or got into difficulties by being reckless or "on tilt".

Q Could you cite any pivotal moments or influences in your early regular betting life that shaped your

style and approach to successful betting?

Lots! The first, and most important, was my belief that an objective approach to betting was more likely to succeed than a subjective one. This was almost the first conclusion I ever drew about betting on horseracing. It came from a cursory glance at the *Sporting Life* Naps Table, which always showed that perhaps only 20% of the racing correspondents showed a profit on their daily "naps". And the really telling condemnation of subjective analysis is that it was always a different 20% of the racing correspondents that managed a profit each year! Reading their columns, I concluded it was because they based their bets on their personal opinion. At that time, I didn't really appreciate the importance of odds in betting, but nevertheless, I have never wavered from my belief in objective analysis from the conclusions drawn as a ten-year-old looking at the *Sporting Life* Naps Table.

Other influences were the speed figures in the *Sporting Chronicle Handicap Book*, the figures of Dick Whitford in *The Sporting Life* (which were my first introduction to the world of collateral form ratings), Phil Bull's *Timeform* Computer Timefigures which I used for ante-post betting on the following year´s Guineas and Derby during the 1980s in particular, and any number of trends that I have found measurable such as the influence of the draw in Flat racing.

Q **My understanding is that you are more a statistically prompted punter than an interpretative one who evaluates form via personal observations. How would you summarize your style?**

As I have alluded to already, the central thread of my betting is objectivity. To summarize this in a sentence, "if I can't measure it, I struggle to evaluate it and so tend to ignore it."

Throughout my betting life I have remained flexible in terms of changing my methods. Over the years I have relied on speed figures, collateral form figures, draw, pace, statistical systems and various mathematical approaches that highlight that most elusive of all variables ... value.

Q What would be a typical betting day for you?

It may surprise you to know that I rarely spend more than half an hour on any meeting. This is because of my objective style of betting. As I rely on figures and statistics and systems, the work has largely been done beforehand. Really, all I require are the runners and an accurate going description. Additional subjective analysis merely results in convergence towards the accepted wisdom, which I constantly strive to avoid. Then I look at Betfair and highlight the potential value horses in each race. It is then a case of deciding the best way to back them.

Q Do you have any particular methods or approaches to handling a bad run of results. Could you give an example of a typical poor run?

The importance of psychology cannot be stressed enough. It is the factor that governs longevity in betting, or indeed any type of investment. When I lived in England I ran a subscription service. I can't recall the year, but during one Flat Season I made a paper profit of just four points to level stakes. In reality, the clients would have lost money because the profits were quoted at prices recommended and these became progressively more difficult to obtain with bookmakers. The meagre profits that year were also due to a 50-1 winner at Royal Ascot and I think the losing sequence prior to that winner was something around 40 points or maybe a little more. That year I lost over half my client base. I recently spoke to a hedge fund manager who operates very similar investment criteria to myself, and he confirmed that he also lost many clients after a poor spell of returns, regardless of past performance. As humans we all share the same psychological response to losses. We time-weigh recent results, so that they have much more influence on our behaviour than past results. Unfortunately, these responses do nothing to help with profitable betting/investment.

Such runs can sap confidence. Nowadays I hardly watch a race, except for the big events. This helps me personally. Watching loser after loser can be soul destroying, you blame bad luck, bad jockeys, bad "anything". If you watch eight losers and then a 10-1 winner, it hardly feels like a profitable day! So, I watch very little racing and sometimes don't even check the results for a few days (I think my record is catching up on four days' worth of results). I actually got that tip from a client. He reasoned that what happened day to day wasn't really of any consequence if you have long-term faith. I think he has a valid point.

Q When someone asks me if I have had a good day, I usually answer "I don't care but I am having a good year." I make this reply not because I wish to be flippant or because it's easy to think this way but because that's where I want to be psychologically. You seem to be there already. Has this always been the case, and more importantly do you think it's innate or can it be developed?

My literal answer to the question is always honest but vague... so something along the lines of "a bit behind", "a bit ahead", "no, not today" or "yes thanks". I'm only vague because I feel it is a little vulgar to mention numbers, akin to mentioning your profit if someone asks about your business. I suppose it also depends on who asks the question.

Therefore I don't think the answer to such a question reflects the broader point you are trying to convey regarding separating the short-term peaks and troughs from the long-term trend in your own mind. I'm lucky on this score because I'm putting faith in rigorous statistics and not in my own ability to find winners; the former is established, the latter is subject to variations in confidence.

Q The betting arena has changed enormously over the last ten years. What impact has this had on your betting?

A huge impact, at one stage I relied almost exclusively on early-morning prices and had accounts with bookmakers all over the country. I visited towns to open accounts with any independent who offered early prices or who might lay me, say, prices offered by the big three or four firms. In the 80s I had a spell on-course to avoid betting tax, but found this soul-destroying. I have just read Dave Nevison's book (very entertaining) in which he states that he prefers being on-course, so there is no right or wrong, but it just wasn't for me. Driving home after losing a four-figure sum made me feel like getting a proper job!

I then discovered the spreads, but restrictions were soon applied and the majority of my bets I placed "abroad" and this was well before Victor moved to Gibraltar! There was quite an underground betting scene and the main reason was to escape the betting tax.

Along came Flutter....my first dalliance with exchanges. They were swallowed up by Betfair and the exchanges changed the betting map of the UK.

Q Some people complain that the exchanges have ruined early-morning value whilst others feel things have never been so good. How do you stand, is it easier to

**make a profit now than before the exchanges?
(Note that profit encompasses all aspects including
getting on.)**

I believe bookmakers have become more astute at identifying winning punters, and at an earlier stage. This makes it difficult to get on and as even accounts in friends and family names, that previously had served you well for a long period of time, are now heavily restricted very early on.

The exchanges are certainly lacking in liquidity in the morning markets. I think this highlights a flaw in the betting exchange business model, which is that eventually you can run out of "layers".

With that caveat, I believe the exchanges have been a positive for punters overall.

Q Do you bet on other sports? How about laying and trading, do they play any significant part in your activities?

I don't trade unless the odds dictate that I should. For example, if I rate something a 14-1 shot and I can back it at 25-1 then I do so. If the price subsequently shortens to 8-1, then I will become a layer and effectively trade that position. But overall, I don't trade.

My main activity nowadays is football betting. The liquidity is much stronger than for horseracing and I find it a new and fascinating challenge. For football, I have joined forces with a really talented partner. The software we use generates prices for all markets (including in-play) and we simply back and lay around those prices. Just as for the racing, it is totally objective, and we aim to become the biggest players in the UK.

Q I am no expert on the football markets, but my guess would be that the bigger profits and turnover is

**within the chaos of in-play betting. I have always
thought the pre-match odds were pretty tight.**

There are anomalies in the pre-match markets, but you are probably
correct that the greater potential for profits occurs during a game,
when the market is constantly changing and reacting to events.
However, the differences are not as marked as I believed they would
be. As with horseracing, certain factors are overlooked or even
misunderstood by the market and this can happen almost as much
pre-match as in-play.

**Q What do you see as the key characteristics needed
in a successful professional gambler?**

Boring stuff really ... being sensible, realistic and brave. But your
greatest ally is belief.

**Q There will always be a nucleus of people
contemplating becoming a full time pro'
in the betting world. What are the positives
and negatives of such a working life style?**

It is no different to running any business of your own. My advice
would be to forget it is about betting ... just treat it as a business. Do
all the things you would do to make any business successful.

**Q How do you balance the demands of professional
gambling with home life? Have you had to make
adjustments over the years and have you at any time
in the past felt like you were simply working too hard
at the betting?**

Some summers have been hard in the past because of the plethora
of racing once the evening meetings kick in. But I have never felt like
I am working too hard.

**Q If I presented to you a willing wannabe professional
who is the type of punter who doesn't lose a lot over
the year but cannot quite break into the regular profit
zone, what advice would you offer them? Are there
any simple tips that might improve the bottom line
by the required amount?**

I couldn't really offer advice unless I knew this punter´s modus
operandi. If we assume he utilizes best prices, exchanges, spreads
etc, but is still not winning, then he needs to change his selection
methods. But a generic piece of advice that we should all have
transplanted into our heads is: It's ALL about the odds, NOTHING
else matters. It is ingrained in punters to try and find the winner of
any race. This is reinforced by the "experts" on TV making a case for/
against a horse, with little, or cursory reference to the odds available.
It is a nonsense of course, but the reality is that a well researched
argument or opinion is far more interesting than a bland statistic.
The opinion makes interesting television, the statistic doesn't.

**Q What are your basic figures, and how long
have you been able to sustain these figures?**

The number of bets depends on the profit margins that I set. For
example, if I set a requirement of a margin of 20% between assessed
price and odds available, I will have fewer bets than if I set the margin
at 10%. If I am aggressive then eight bets per meeting would be an
average. Strike-rate also varies with the levels of margin set, but a
broad average would be between 15 and 18%. This has been relatively
consistent over the years, though I am always a little surprised by the
amount of variation season to season.

Football betting is a different animal. There are fewer unknown
variables and so I can price up all markets and have a back and

lay price for ALL selections. Therefore the number of bets on an individual game can run into three figures.

Q What is the worst bet you ever made – gory details included please!

The year Seagram won the Grand National, I had my biggest ever bet on Garrison Savannah. At that time, I was heavily into ante-post betting and I had backed Garrison at all prices, I think from 25-1 to 10-1. I would have won enough to buy a terraced house, so the equivalent of £100,000 today. The scale of the bet was due to a theory I have about the Grand National, which has brought me numerous winners of the race. On the day, I didn't even watch the race ... I was at Sincil Bank watching Lincoln City. People in the crowd had radios on and I asked a chap behind me, quite nonchalantly, who had won the National? "They're just coming to the last", he said ... "Garrison Savannah has gone ten lengths clear". I kept really cool and started dreaming of my winnings. A minute later the chap patted me on the shoulder and said "Seagram won it". Deflated wasn't the word!

When I got home I watched the race on video. If any of you can recall the race, Garrison jumps past Seagram at the last and quickly powers ten lengths clear ... at this stage, had Betfair been around, he would have been 1.01! As I watched the video, I couldn't believe that somehow this horse would get beat. But, at the elbow, he simply died, like Crisp had done years before.

Certainly my worst betting experience.

Q Is most of your daily selection process automated, even down to the selection of value, or do you have to resort to some manual analysis?

In horseracing, 95% is automated, but some things I just find easier to assess manually than trying to assign a numerical value to.

In football, 95% is automated. Even the team news prior to kick-off generates an automatic numerical indication of the effect it will have on goal expectations. However, to do that player ratings are required and they are a mixture of Opta stats and watching every Premiership game each week ... so that is the 5% manual analysis.

Q You live abroad now, how has this affected you on a personal quality of life level and on a betting level?
We have lived in Spain for four years and now four years in Dubai. Moving to a new country brings frustrations, but overall we have enjoyed the experiences. It has exposed my family and myself to different cultures and other ways of life.

On the betting front, it has taken me even further away from consensus opinion as I no longer have the *Racing Post* or other mainstream publications drip-feeding me opinions. Whether this has been positive or negative in terms of profitability is difficult to tell, but it has certainly made decisions more clear cut.

The technology of today means that geographical distance isn't really an issue.

INTERVIEWED IN JANUARY 2008

Chapter 5

RICHARD HOILES

Richard Hoiles is well known as a racing commentator but also flagged, by those who recognize punting nous, as someone with a good command of what is required to make a betting profit. For me he will always be the guy who was shouted down by Big Mac when he tried to introduce the topic of odds lines on "The Morning Line" the day Swain won one of his King Georges. It was a day when Mac confirmed, if it was needed, that he knows little about successful betting whilst Richard was clearly someone worth keeping an eye and ear on.

Q. How did you first get interested in racing and betting?

My dad used to watch the ITV 7 on a Saturday but it wasn't until we went to Plumpton one day and went and stood by the open ditch that the size and speed of it all hooked me.

I loved charts and numbers as a kid and so form fascinated me. I have diaries full of selections, profit and losses from the age of thirteen so a few of the hard lessons were learnt without actually parting with any real money.

Q What other jobs have you been involved in and how did you move into TV?

I am a qualified cost and management accountant. I qualified early and moved up pretty quickly until during the last recession in the early 1990s firms were suddenly employing slightly older people rather than aggressive analysts from lots of entrepreneurial firms that had gone bust!

I answered an ad in the old *Sporting Life* for commentators but was so naïve I didn't even realize you needed to send in a tape. Fortunately the rejection letter (which I still have) and my demo crossed in the post and SIS were good enough to give me a trial, which led to me getting a contract.

TV followed with the launch of The Racing Channel three years later. I will always be so grateful that George Irvine and Mick Embleton were prepared to give someone with no experience a chance. I hope I have repaid their faith.

Q How would you describe your early punting career and your progress through to profitable betting?

I actually made a profit from quite early on but we are talking small stakes so there were none of the difficulties of getting on or pressures of having to win a decent amount each month.

My fixation with recording every bet meant I took losses, however small, personally and would only bet on track, priding myself on getting the biggest price. My obsession with numbers and the losses from those early diaries (where there had been selections in every race) had taught me well.

Q **What were the pivotal influences over the years that transformed your betting?**

Reading books such as *Beyer On Speed* and Steve Davidowitz's *Betting Thoroughbreds* helped widen my knowledge.

Mark Coton's Value Betting really struck a chord and I spent a fair amount of time learning how to construct tissues, private handicaps and speed figures.

Learning how to do these yourself teaches you the mechanics, where they work and don't work and whose figures you trust and whose you don't. I don't do any of these regularly now, there is just too much racing and too little time, but it gave me confidence that I could use the right information in the right circumstances.

My biggest influence was undoubtedly working in Hong Kong and doing video form for one of the betting syndicates. Each horse was assessed against 30 specific criteria and you could never do a race properly in less than an hour. The computer was capable of modelling the key criteria as well as the compiler's strengths and weaknesses. My strength was sectional times and the fact they are not in place on the all-weather in this country still frustrates! Learning the best and worst tactical positions for various tempos and track biases would prove invaluable for in-running many years later.

Finally I worked for five years with jockey Felix Coetzee doing speed maps for every race and talking through race tactics. It was a really rare opportunity to work with one of the top riders in the world, who had the confidence and trust to follow our plans whilst being prepared to improvise when things did not pan out as anticipated. By the end of our time I felt I was sitting on his shoulder in races, I knew him so well, and it means I can happily dismiss criticisms that I 'have never ridden'. A top jockey, and the success we had remains, outside commentating, my proudest achievement.

Q Could you give us an illustration of a speed map, perhaps for a single past race, that illustrates the technique.

Write horses out in draw order and then assign points to each based on their positions in their previous five starts. In Hong Kong and the States this is easy as the actual run positions are printed in the form but in this country you have to be a bit more flexible. I allocate up to three points plus or minus for each start so a horse that has led on each of its last five starts would get +15 and one that says held up in rear would get -15. Comments such as prominent would be +2, held up towards rear -2, chased/tracked leaders usually +1, held up -1, and midfield 0.

The point is that while utmost precision can be achieved afterwards by reviewing the videos of the last five runs, the idea is to quickly find races that have a potential tempo angle, or where if there's an even pace some horses drawn wide who do not go forward or back will be trapped wide.

Put a scale across the bottom from +15 to -15 then starting with the horse closest to the rail position mark where they are likely to be after two furlongs based on the points allocated. If a horse has a similar number of points it will be positioned one off the fence, then two off and so on.

Q Is there a particular starting point that shapes your approach to analyzing a race?

A strong view either positive or negative. Trust your opinion and be prepared to make or lose money on it.

Too many fritter money away on races that they do not have a strong view on, or worse still rely on somebody else's.

Q **What are the betting tools that you utilize to analyze a race?**

My own notes held on *Raceform Interactive*, *Timeform* ratings, speed maps on the Flat and trainer form are the main components.

Maintaining lists of horses of interest and the ability to have them flagged when they are declared is the main starting point for races to initially look at.

Q **You mention trainer form, do you mean simply whether a trainer's horses are running well recently or are you referring to other types of "form"? If so could you give an example?**

The current form the trainer's horses are in. I use the *Post*'s feature Today's Trainers for this and add the win and placed column for runners over the past two weeks and compare it to the total number of runners. If 50% of a trainer's runners (minimum sample size five) have won or placed they are on my list of trainers currently in good form and their horses are upgraded.

Any trainer on a losing run of 20 or more has their runners downgraded. I then keep a record by trainer of dates they were in and out of form to help remind me of the reason their horses may have run well or badly at that time, which is easily forgotten months later.

A little goldmine is small trainers who jump from the out-of-form to in-form list, such as Chris Gordon recently. Once their purple patch has finished they will usually struggle again because their horses are too high in the weights.

Q **What do you see as the key characteristics needed in a successful professional gambler?**

Discipline is for me the key. If you record all your bets from an early stage and concentrate on specific areas you can still find an edge.

Not being too greedy or believing in your own infallibility are other lessons that strike a chord!

The other thing is to move with the times. In the old days it was very time consuming to research a horse's record so a preference for soft ground or a certain trip was only apparent after slogging through lots of form books. With horses' career records now displayed at the touch of a button such an edge has disappeared and the same is true of many other factors that are now discounted by the market. Track and tempo biases have become increasingly important because of the fact they still are hard to reflect in black and white form comments and so I think they still provide an edge, but you should always be on the lookout for or exploring new variables.

Q Do you think the media helps or hinders the punter? Who would you recommend reading or listening to?

I always watch racing with the sound off but record it all. If I am wrong about a particular race then I will often listen back to the views of others to see if they mention something I missed or did not factor in highly enough.

I am lucky in working with pundits regularly so know who can back up their selections with solid reasoning. Eddie Fremantle, Steve Mellish and Graham Cunningham are always great company and a fertile source of things to ponder.

The media should help in offering sparks to ignite your own interest and help with the learning process. After that it should always be down to you. Taking responsibility for your own bets rather than blaming others is still something too many are not prepared to do.

Q Any advice on coping with the inevitable losing run?

The hardest question of all!

My records show that in 1990 I had a run of 23 losers despite my average price being around 5-1. About three from the end of that sequence I had backed a horse called Ryde Again, a stamina-laden horse against old boy Floyd, a front runner who was at that stage very doubtful at three miles.

When Ryde Again took over between the last two I could not help let out all the frustration and was roaring him home when to my horror Floyd rallied and got back up. I was so shattered mentally I went home, and didn't back a horse in the last that won.

When the sequence was finally broken by a horse winning by 30 lengths at Lingfield I fully expected it to either fall at the last or some Act of God to befall it up the run-in, so low was my confidence.

Eight of the next thirteen won and now that list of losers and winners is a regular source of solace when things are not going to plan.

Q What form do your actual bets take?

In-running from home forms the basis nowadays simply because the records show that is what I am best at. It often overlaps into taking positions prior to the race based on run styles, tempo angles or horses' own idiosyncrasies.

In the past it was always win only unless the shape of the market gave thieving each-way potential.

I am more active in ante-post markets now due to the ability to trade and given my boring accountant's background I am never afraid to lock in a profit!

Q What kind of technology are you using for in-running from home?

Nothing special, I use Gruss but nowhere near to its full capabilities. Minimizing mistakes in hitting the wrong buttons is a key part of in-running so I am happy to compromise speed to some degree for an element of safety.

Clearly picture delays mean I am not playing in the closing stages of a race however appealing the odds may seem – there is a reason!

Q How difficult is it to balance the demands of punting and pundit work with the rest of your life?

Since Jack's arrival a couple of years ago increasingly difficult! The benefit of in-running is that it relies on good race-reading skills more than anything so is easier to do with less preparation.

I have always found it easy to separate work days from betting days. The margins are too small to give betting anything less than your full attention. Work days are very much spent identifying horses of interest for the future and I will often stay in the commentary box all afternoon watching racing from everywhere that day to try and keep in touch.

Q Finally, if I presented to you a willing wannabe professional who is the type of punter who doesn't lose a lot over the year but cannot quite break into the regular profit zone, what advice would you offer them? Are there any simple tips that might improve the bottom line by the required amount?

Firstly I would point out that if you are not losing much you are doing far better than most, so have confidence you are doing a lot right.

Check you are recording all your bets and being hard on yourself in analyzing your losses. Are your bank management and staking plan reflective of the strength of your opinion? Too many play too often just because they need the buzz or can't stand the thought of a horse they like winning unbacked.

Betting in fewer races means you can watch the others more effectively, finding a future winner in a race you did not have a bet in is far more productive in the long run.

Q You mention staking plans, what staking plan do you adopt with your own betting?

Generally backing or laying to win a certain amount with three tiers. The top amount is clearly races where I have the strongest view, medium is where I believe there is a clearly identifiable angle to exploit and small is really an action bet just to give me some interest and to stop me getting frustrated and going on tilt if something I feel should have backed wins.

Staking ratio would be action bets 2% of maximum, medium 25% of maximum.

Q Finally, what are your ambitions in life generally and specifically racing/betting?

My initial ambition, having been lucky enough to get a job in the sport I genuinely love, was to be able to do it at whatever level until I felt I was no longer good enough.

The experiences I have had and races I have been lucky enough to have called have far exceeded my expectations. My objective is to always try to convey enthusiasm and back up any arguments with clear reasoning to allow constructive analysis afterwards of where things went right, or more often wrong. If you are conducting an experiment and you know what you expect to happen then it is far easier to correctly interpret the results.

My remaining ambition is to stand at the open ditch at Plumpton, long after having retired, and still get the same buzz as I did all those years ago.

INTERVIEWED IN MARCH 2010

Chapter 6

TOM SEGAL (PRICEWISE)

No introductions needed here. Tom is one of the main tipsters behind Pricewise, in fact the stats show that he is probably the main profitable influence behind the members' section of this service. On main race days he can be found offering free Pricewise selections in the *Racing Post*.

Q How did you first get interested in racing and betting?

I lived right next to Sandown Park, so went racing a lot and caught the bug.

Q What other jobs have you been involved in and how did you move into journalism/tipping?

After university I worked for *Raceform* for a few years, when they were based at Weatherbys. I then joined the *Racing Post* what must be nearly 15 years ago now. In other words I haven't done anything else.

Q How would you describe your early punting career and your progress through to profitable betting?

I wouldn't describe my early punting career as anything because I wasn't interested. I liked the sport and still do, much prefer it to betting, but discovered quite quickly that I was quite good at spotting a good horse. I Started backing a few ante-post winners of the big races and have stuck to that mantra ever since. I don't bet on the crap because I'm no good at it. Stick to the major meetings at the major tracks.

Q What were the pivotal influences over the years that transformed your betting?

Betting was never in the forefront of my mind, still isn't, I find it much more rewarding to find the winner of a big race before anyone else than any financial gain. Consequently I don't think there have been any influences at all. I don't use figures of any kind, I don't listen to pundits ever and quite simply I just watch the good races lots of times. My ability, if I have one, is spotting a good horse before anyone else and acting upon that. In fact I would go so far as to say that the reason most punters lose is because they don't trust their instincts enough and use others' instead.

Q Is there a particular starting point that shapes your approach to analyzing a race?

Not really. Obviously my job is price related so nine times out of ten I'm looking to oppose those at the front of the market, but I don't have a magic way in. I simply get the internet fired up and watch as many of the horses involved in the race as many times as I can. Having said that jockeys are my big thing and I strongly believe that they are the most important factor in any race after the ability of the horse. For example I would always consider the booking of Ruby Walsh a massive plus and Tony McCoy an even bigger negative.

Q Would Tony McCoy be a negative because he is overbet or are you referring to his riding ability?

Riding ability. I deal in big races and he doesn't win many. He wouldn't be in my top ten current jockeys.

Q What are the betting tools that you utilize to analyze a race?

Watching replays of past races and the prices.

Q What do you see as the key characteristics needed in a successful professional gambler?

I'm certainly not a professional gambler. I would have about a hundred bets a year, if that, the Betfair boys would have that many in half a day but the key is to find a method that suits your temperament best and to concentrate on that. Irish racing suits me because not only are most of the best Flat horses there but also they only have about five meetings a week. Good quality racing in a manageable size, perfect.

Q Do you think the media helps or hinders the punter? Who would you recommend reading or listening to?

To be honest I wouldn't have a clue how to answer this one because I don't read opinions or watch TV racing very often. My guess is that they are a hindrance to many punters but only the casual ones who don't really care if they win or lose, as most punters will have their own opinions.

Listen, I wouldn't recommend anyone because what suits my way of reading a race would be different for most others. Personally I'm a James Willoughby fan.

Q If you are a James Willoughby fan there must be a reason for this, could you outline what those reasons are?

His way of thinking about racing is different from most. I'm not interested in any quantifiable method of assessing a race and he strikes me as a bloke who is looking at factors away from the mainstream.

Q Any advice on coping with the inevitable losing run?

Nope. If you try your best what more can you do? If you are having stupid bets, then don't.

Q What form do your personal bets take?

Straight win with the bookies. I don't even have a Betfair account.

Q If your 100 bets a year are away from the front of the market I am surprised you don't have a Betfair account in order to maximise your profit. Is there a more fundamental reason for no Betfair?

Yes there is but I'm not prepared to expand on that.

Q How difficult is it to balance the demands of punting and newspaper work with the rest of your life?

I don't punt very much so that is not a problem but with two young kids working weekends can be a chore. Having said that I do work from home so I see them all the time and there are worse jobs than mine, that's for sure. As long as I can get to see Reading on a Saturday I'm happy.

Q **Finally, if I presented to you a willing wannabe professional who is the type of punter who doesn't lose a lot over the year but cannot quite break into the regular profit zone, what advice would you offer them? Are there any simple tips that might improve the bottom line by the required amount?**

That's a hard one because most punters find a method that suits them and tend to stick with it. However I would say that many middle-of-the-road punters tend to be scared of a big price and tend to have too many bad-value bets at short prices that make little difference whether they win or lose. However I wouldn't be any authority on what makes a good punter or not.

Q **When you started out as Pricewise, how confident were you that you could produce the goods? Did you receive any advice from your predecessor?**

I didn't really think about it. Of course there is a professional pride but I'd been a sort of understudy for a few years and done reasonably well. It suits my style because I only have to look at races with quality horses in them.

No. Mel Collier's methods and mine would be like chalk and cheese.

Q **You say Mel Collier's methods and yours are chalk and cheese, could you expand on that a little?**

You'd have to speak to Mel about his methods, but most punters/tipsters I've come across are figures based. I'm most certainly not and wouldn't care one iota about any rating or speed figure a horse may have.

Q Do you or the *Racing Post* keep past records of Pricewise selections and could these be published?

No I don't keep records, just lazy.

Q Finally, What are your ambitions in life generally and specifically racing/betting?

Be happy in both.

INTERVIEWED IN APRIL 2010

Chapter 7

MARK LAYDEN

Mark Layden runs the highly successful SystematicBetting.com advisory service. He is not only a professional punter but a university lecturer in computer science. He has graduated (no pun intended) from the academic world into the world of professional punting over the last ten to fifteen years.

Q Hi Mark, thank you for doing the interview. Can we start by finding out a little about you and how you got involved in betting?

I was introduced to racing back in 1976 by a friend at college. The inevitable happened in that I had 3 x 50p doubles and a 50p treble and they all won. I was initially captured by the excitement of big group races and that year I remember Wollow and Flying Water winning the Guineas but it was a colt with four white socks named The Minstrel that I fell in love with. Thankfully I was kicked out of college after one year and therefore never became a PE and Maths teacher. I went on later to do a degree in computer science. I worked for a year down south with IBM but got the teaching bug again whilst doing a bit of night school teaching near Winchester. This prompted me to go back into teaching after my degree. I realized that I like playing sports but not necessarily teaching them. By contrast I did find teaching computing stimulating. These days I live in the Midlands with my long-suffering partner and our fifteen-year-old son.

Q How long did it take you before you became a profitable bettor and was there a breakthrough moment?

Over the years I was pretty much a break-even punter, the winning years probably reflecting how much time I put in, but looking back I can see that my early perception of betting was flawed. My betting was governed too much by my interest, so my bets tended to be on high-class races with very few in handicaps. I also did not fully appreciate the concept of value and the fact that your bets somehow have to utilize an angle or opinion not commonly held by the crowd. During the 1990s I did very little betting as I was university lecturing and owning/running a restaurant. Around the year 2000 however, I realized that betting conditions had become so favourable for punters that I rolled my sleeves up and became immersed in the sport once again. This time I was rubbing shoulders with some clued-up players on the old *Smartsig* forum and your way of thinking about betting soon reshapes. The breakthrough moment was in the year 2000 when I realized that a statistical approach to betting could be both objective and profitable. Becoming successful also made me realize that the majority of media pundits don't know what they are talking about so I would suggest ignoring the mass media. Let's face it, even if they spoke a little sense the fact is that every other punter is listening in.

Q How did you go about making your selections when you first began betting and how do you make them now? Has there been a lot of change?

In my early years I would be like any other punter. Starting with commonly available numbers such as Topspeed and betting accordingly. Looking back now I realize that you are going to find it hard to make it pay using commonly accessible numbers in a conventional way. Today my selections are based on statistical trends and take me about half an hour to produce my daily list each day. I have to maintain a database of racing data to keep my trend analysis up to date and I think my ability and background in programming has helped me to perform analysis that goes beyond the widely available packages such as Racing Systems Builder or *Raceform Interactive*. Once I have made my selections it's then all about the price. I concentrate on getting the best odds that I can and I am on above SP around 73% of the time. If there is one simple piece of advice I would give to other more casual punters it would be find out how much you are beating SP by and do you shop round for prices; if not then you should start.

Q What factors do you consider when you analyze a race or is it dependent on the race?

Some angles are race dependent but the majority apply to any race. One thing I would say from personal experience is forget the well worn theory that one should avoid lower-grade races. It's total hogwash – although I accept that a person's approach might be better suited to more valuable races, the idea that everyone should stay clear of lower-grade racing is complete rubbish. One thing I will say that might surprise a few people is that the going plays absolutely no part in my daily thoughts. Most days I don't even know what the going is.

Q Do you think that you need to have certain personality traits to be able to make a long-term profit from betting, and what would they be?

Most certainly YES. You need patience for sure and that old chestnut discipline. I liken betting to hang gliding. You spend what seems like quite long periods going nowhere or even dropping down and then you catch a thermal and, whoosh, you are suddenly elevated to a higher position than you occupied a few months ago. Most punters are only capable of viewing their punting through a small window, so for them they are either having a good day or week or a poor one. If it's poor they get disillusioned and change tack or pack it in. Last year I had a sensational first six months and the next six months I broke even, resulting in a very good year overall. The key is the second six months, most people would not be able to get up and keep going through the motions. Having said that I don't want too many six-month stagnant periods. Maybe computer programmers make good gamblers – after all they spend most of their time getting it wrong in order to eventually get it right.

Q Do you use systematic betting or more of a form analysis approach, and what would you say are the good and bad points of each?

I use the former. The benefit of the former is the objectivity it brings to the daily bets and that objectivity is a godsend when it's not going so well. The advantage to the latter is that a skilful exponent will always outperform the systematic bettor but on the down side he will probably have to spend more daily time achieving it.

**Q How often do you update your methods,
and do you find that it is a full-time job
or do you have time for other things?**

I am constantly putting ideas and approaches on the betting back-burner. If I feel they are rigorous enough I will start betting them to half stakes and feel my way in. I suppose my constant analysis is the equivalent of the form reader's form and video analysis.

**Q What kind of bankroll, in terms of units,
do you work with and do you prefer to flat bet
or use some other kind of staking method?**

I am not particularly aggressive with my money management. My feelings are that most money management theory tends to forget the psychological factor and of course this differs from person to person. I started off with a bank of 60 points, which looking back was a little light considering I bet one point level stakes win only off a strike rate of about 28%. At the end of the year I upped my stakes but only such that I was now betting 100th of my bank. Reviewing at the end of the year was something I did for about the first six years and then I changed to every six months, but reducing the percentage of bank whilst increasing the bet size to the point where I suppose my bet size is now about 1000th of my bank. From this you can see that I have not been terribly aggressive but you also have to remember that there is a limit to how much you can physically get on and that side of things is getting tougher.

**Q You mentioned losing periods, any advice on
how to cope with them?**

Keeping past records is the key as they offer you comfort during the poor times. One trick I have is to simply pin a piece of paper on the wall which details past poor periods. In my office the wall has a piece of paper which has "IT'S HAPPENED BEFORE, 5th December 2005 243 bets -49 points" as one of its documented periods. Reminding oneself of these past periods helps you get through the current poor run. I do not believe in taking a break or scaling down. For me it's keep going and work your way through and out of it.

Q **When did you first become involved with *SmarterSig* and how did you end up being the editor?**

I joined in 2000 and was a member until it went belly up around 2007. Becoming the editor of the reformed *SmarterSig* was a bit of an accident. As the old *SmartSig* was looking to go web-based I volunteered to set up an email discussion list as an interim measure until the web facility came online from the previous owner. It never appeared and in fact *SmartSig* disappeared. We kept the email list going for about 18 months and then someone suggested I should restart the magazine. I was thinking about it when Justin Penrose submitted an article to the list and I thought, yes I miss this sort of stuff and I am pretty sure others do too. I relaunched *SmarterSig* in January 2008.

Q **What can be gained by reading the *SmarterSig* magazine?**

I think its absolutely invaluable and I would say that even if we were still running under the old *SmartSig* and I was just a subscriber. It's not just about information and betting angles, although there are plenty of those to read and discuss. The most important thing is that you are talking to successful punters with a wide range of expertise. Their outlook on betting rubs off on you without you even noticing it. There is an old saying that your wealth is usually equivalent to the average of your six closest friends. The same applies to betting. If you mix with successful players there is a far greater chance of you becoming one. Let me give you a concrete example. When I first joined *SmartSig back* in 2000 I couldn't understand why the discussion forum didn't buzz the day before the Derby or some top Group 1 at Royal Ascot. I quickly realized that these people are interested in sensible investment strategies and not propping up the enjoyment of a top race with a personal bet.

Q Is *SmarterSig* for experienced bettors or is it as useful for new bettors?

I think anyone can gain benefit from it. Throughout the last ten years I have always noticed how sympathetic and helpful other members are to anyone who comes along and clearly demonstrates that they are towards the foot of the learning curve.

Q Did *SmarterSig* help you in making a profit or were you already profitable by that time?

The pivotal influences for me were firstly appreciating that it's how the other punter thinks that I have to factor into my betting. Alan Potts' book *Against the Crowd* helped here. Secondly the statistical approach was probably influenced by Russell Clarke's writings and some American authors. The third major influence was *SmartSig* and its members.

Q You now run the advisory service www. systematicbetting.com. Does this put a different slant on picks given that your are advising clients?

Not really, I back whatever the clients are advised so when things are going poorly it's the same for me.

Q Are you involved in any other form of betting?

I have some software that I have written that automatically analyses and lays in the win market and place bets in the place market. I see my own betting gradually moving over to a fully automated approach as I get older. There comes a point when chasing round bookmakers is for younger legs. I also like the idea of letting these things run and simply checking them once a week to see how things are going. Successful betting should be a means to an end and if it does not buy time for you then perhaps personal values need to be re-examined. Football betting interests me but I simply do not have the time to juggle this along with the racing. Having said that a friend of mine has just finished a PhD in the statistical modeling of football outcomes and I am trying to persuade him to go into business on this front.

Q Could you give readers any pointers towards areas where an edge can be found?

What I would say is forget the rubbish the media throws out, whether it be this horse is 3lb better off or this race has thrown up two winners and three seconds since it was run. These are all well observed by other punters and quite frankly of little use as a means of finding betting value. Pace analysis would be a good area to focus on and develop your expertise, it is relatively ignored in this country. On a more general theme I would suggest likening your betting to fishing. I would imagine most anglers want to know where in the river fish stocks are congregating. Do the same with betting. Find out what types of horse or race characteristics cost the punter most and avoid them. If you are currently losing 10% on your turnover then start by finding out how you can reduce this to 5%. For many punters this may be simply making sure they walk across the road and take 11-4 instead of 5-2. Of course the above assumes you know what your yearly losses are and this would be the golden rule that all successful punters will advise. Log your bets and ensure that you can analyze them in a meaningful way. If you are not prepared to do this then accept you are never going to make it.

Q What are your medium- to long-term ambitions with your betting?

I am getting more involved with purely automated betting on Betfair using software of my own. I think there will come a point in time when I want to do less at the PC and simply check the account status every week or month, and automated betting is the vehicle for this. This means gradually moving my betting and laying over to an automated platform which I am currently doing. Betting on Betfair will mean pre-off time betting only which in turn will mean a lower return on investment percentage but if I crank up the amount of action I am happy with this kind of trade in. We have to try and remember that we bet to live not live to bet. Doing the latter probably gets you to where you want to be financially but there comes a point when you need to generally take stock of life and get things in perspective.

INTERVIEWED IN JULY 2010

Chapter 8

NICK AUBREY

INTERVIEW BY DAVE DUFFIELD

This chapter was kindly provided by Dave Duffield who interviewed the successful Australian punter Nick Aubrey.

Q You're an actuary by trade – how much of a part does your mathematics background play in your approach to betting?

This depends on why I am betting. If I go to the track to have a social day and not worry if I win or lose then I will bet small but pick my selections on a whim, for example I might like the sire of an unraced two-year-old so I'll back it. But if I am betting to win money and because I am a technical punter (as opposed to a form-based punter) and my approach is based on probability theory then knowing the maths is THE most important aspect of my operation. If you continually get better odds then the "true" odds then you WILL win in the long term. Conversely if you continually accept worse odds then you will lose in the long term. A commonly held view is that "any price is a good price about a winner" but this can only be true after the event.

Q How do you go about determining your selections?

I probably spent about 20 years off and on trying to develop the best ratings system. I used neural networks, fuzzy logic and linear programming to come up with my best bets for the day. On a Friday night I would get excited about a horse I rated at 3-1 that the overnight price for was 10-1. I went to the track and immediately went to its box to make sure it had arrived okay and that it looked ready to win. I then went to the betting ring as soon as betting opened for the race only to discover that the bookies opened it at 5-2. By that stage I had an emotional attachment with the horse so I still backed it even though I knew it was no longer value. I have kept stats on every bet I ever made ("if you give an actuary an inch he will measure it") and found I was making about +4% on turnover. After deducting expenses for the day plus time spent my ROI (Return On Investment) was negative. I then realized that everyone else's form study/inside knowledge/track bias/horse fitness on the day culminates in the prices being offered on each runner just before the off. Then along came the Internet and so why bother spending time and effort doing work that has already been done for you? I am now a non-form punter and have consistently been earning +15% profit on turnover with minimal effort, and my ROI has gone through the roof.

Q What do you think are the most important factors to consider when having a bet?

Price, price and price.

Q How many bets would you have in a day/week/month?

It depends upon the number of anomalies identified. Using my U-BET software I can operate every day of the week even though I may be working, playing golf or playing with the kids but some days there are no value bets identified. If I had to spend eight hours in front of a computer and not have one single bet then I would go mad. Other days there can be up to 20 bets. When an exotics anomaly is detected (pre-race expected return of at least 110%) I will place a large bet of up to 8,000 combinations with bet size being determined using my Dutch Book formula.... after the race the return will be anything from +400% to -100% ; somewhat paradoxically exotics provide me with my most consistent returns.

Q Do you find it easier to make a profit on metropolitan meetings or the country/provincials?

Without doubt the best value bets can be found at the country/ provincials. The trick is to secure the best price. A couple of years ago a few corporate bookies were offering the best of three TABs (Totalisator Agency Board prices) on all races and accepting bets until jump time and our profits were excellent. Because we were winning consistently they quickly closed or stymied our accounts stating that they only cater for "recreational punters". But they subsequently changed their rules and now only offer the best of three on metro race meetings.

Q How much effort do you put into getting best odds on your bets?

Getting the best price is the most important part so this is where 80% of my time is spent. TwoNix U-Bet software (www.twonix. com) allows users to lodge bets at the best price available at, say, ten seconds before race start. Bets on many runners in the same race can be placed on New South Wales, Victoria or Queensland TABs or IAS fixed odds or SP and all this can happen in the last ten seconds before jump. Getting the best price available will increase the punter's POT by around 10% so it can turn a losing 5% POT system into one that wins 5%.

Q Do you bet the exotics or just win only?

Both ... estimating exotic returns is difficult as there are generally no approximates available. But the rewards can be exceptional. Many pro punters I know only bet exotics and especially when there are jackpots. A jackpot exotic is the only investment I know where a company will give back more money than they have been given for that event. For example a $50k jackpot with $100k new money might return 80% of ($50k + $100k) = $120k = 20% extra money being returned. Of course you have to get the exotic but that's where knowing Dutch Book maths comes in handy.

Q Track bias has dominated the headlines recently – how do you factor it into your form assessment?

It's irrelevant to the way I bet. If track bias is correctly reflected in the price offered then that's okay. If it's not and track bias influenced the result then the winner will pay better than it should have ... and you don't get paid on losers.

Q What are the main skills that you think are required by someone who wants to be a successful pro punter?

I can only talk for my own punting style which is technical. For me the human factor is the hardest to overcome. It's easy to analyze what your results should have been after the event. The trick is to be able to operate your system correctly before the race.

My own punting maxims are:

1. Plan your bets (both selections and staking) and then stick to your plan.
2. Probability has no memory.
3. Don't worry about short-term losses – even pro punters have long losing runs; punting success has to be measured over the long term.
4. Probability has no memory.
5. For technical punters, study and pass Probability Theory 101
6. For form punters, pick the factors that you want to specialize in (e.g. Geoff Hutson's pre-race behaviour) and then become an expert on the subject. Form punters can only win if they have an edge over the rest of the market.
7. Probability has no memory.

Q Do you bet on sports as well or just the races?

Yes I bet on sports but more for fun. I tend to be an emotional punter when it comes to sports betting. I backed Lleyton Hewitt when he won 2002 Wimbledon but mainly to enhance the "Aussie done good" experience rather than trying to make money. But with the advent of Betfair I have been doing sports trading rather than sports betting. For example in test cricket I will lay a draw before a ball is bowled and then close out once I have made a 20% profit. Even if the game does end in a draw the price will almost always fluctuate sufficiently to make 20% on your money. Already on the first Ashes test (started 23/11/06) you could have laid the draw at 4.00 and then backed it at 4.80 thus ensuring a 20% profit.

Q Where do you see the racing industry in say five years?

I recently attended the AJC wagering forum where there were some very astute and interesting speakers. Most agreed that the racing industry has had it good for the last 50 years but that unless significant changes were made quickly there is a real risk that the racing industry will be lost to future generations. I happened to visit the Sydney Hyde Park War Memorial the other day and was reading a newspaper printed on the day WWII ended. The front page had instructions that workers can have tomorrow off but would be expected to front for work on Friday. It also mentioned that there would be a special race meeting held at Canterbury Park the next day to celebrate the end of WWII. There is no doubt that racing is in the psyche of most Australians. Where else do they have a race that stops the nation? Many would argue that a crowd of 128,000 on Derby Day indicates a healthy industry but the reality is quite different. At the wagering forum Con Kafataris (Centrebet) calls it the Boozy Floozie syndrome in that many of the younger people don't get to see a single horse race live ... watching it on the big screen is as close as they get. In my humble opinion we have to get them emotionally involved and offer more than just pub TAB facilities. At the wagering forum Bill Saunders (Cyberhorse) presented some great ideas about how to woo back the lost generation and hopefully the racing administrators will act on some of these. For what it's worth my idea is as follows ...

Why not offer every person on course the opportunity to become an owner for the day. The idea is that a patron pays an extra $20 entrance fee for which they randomly get a horse card for the day. This card shows them all the details about their horse and entitles them to owner privileges such as going to see their horse in the stable area, talking to the real owners and strapper plus one day-owner per horse gets access to the bird-cage enclosure where they can talk with the trainer and hear instruction being given to the jockey. After the race if the horse wins then the day-owners win some prize money by virtue of the original $20 payment collected from all day-owners. At least then every race would be well supported ... vocally. This would create an emotional attachment between racegoer and horse which would flow over to future race days where past day-owners would be interested in how the horse they owned a few weeks ago is going. Later on they may even purchase their own share of a racehorse.

Q What do you think are the main reasons why most punters fail?

Pot of gold mentality: Most casual punters want to win big from a meagre outlay. An economic theory is that profit is a reward for risk bearing ... the more risk you take the bigger the profits but also the bigger the chance of losses.

The herd mentality: Many casual punters don't have enough confidence in their own punting abilities and so will follow the herd ... by backing other people's tips or backing a runner AFTER it has shortened in considerably. They don't appreciate that the average punter loses 16% on turnover so unless they become a non-average punter they will also lose 16%.

Progressive staking: A punter may have done years and years of research using millions of past races as the basis of his system rules. He then puts his hard earned down to discover that from his first 500 bets he has lost -50% rather than winning his predicted +20%. He tries to bet his way out of trouble by increasing his bets. Initially this works but he has another bad run which wipes out his bank. He failed because he didn't understand that progressive staking will greatly increase the risk of ruin.

Q You often talk about "risk of ruin". Tell us how it applies to punting?

Understanding "risk of ruin" helps punters appreciate how bad luck affects both winning and losing systems and that there can be no guarantee your profit will be consistently produced. For example my best performing system is a non-form based system called 5P. Overall 5P managed to win +23% POT warts and all over a 12-month period. But this was made up of two quarters where we won +12% POT, one quarter -1% POT but the other quarter was +60% POT. Before my first bet I knew that given a strike rate of 17% over 2,000 bets we were going to have a run of outs of around 33. Well we had 32 consecutive losers (in the losing quarter) but also had three runs of three consecutive winners. Winning isn't about backing winners, it's about getting the best price on every single bet. The winners will come along when they are good and ready. My "risk of ruin" calculator (available for free at www.twonix.com) helps to illustrate the inconsistent nature of punting.

Chapter 9

STEVE LEWIS HAMILTON

Steve Lewis Hamilton is a racing tipster and TV pundit. He was one of around six tipsters reviewed over a period of time by the *Guardian* newspaper in an investigation into whether it was possible to make money following tipsters. We met up in Chesterfield where he now lives and had a most enjoyable interview, often drifting off topics to chat and exchange views on racing and betting generally. On behalf of himself and his clients he clearly works hard at his betting.

Q Steve, tell me a little about how you first got involved with racing.

I first wanted to be a professional footballer and had spells with quite a few London clubs, spending most of my playing days at Millwall. This didn't work out for me and although I kept on playing semi-pro with the likes of Bromley coupled with some evening coaching,

I still needed to supplement my income and it was at this time that I took an afternoon job at a bookmakers and also worked early mornings at Smithfield meat market. I met a guy at the bookmakers who introduced me to the notion that form study involved more than just *The Sporting Life*. He showed me how to use a form book and basically added some structure to the way I looked at betting.

Q Was he a pro punter?

No, he was the shop manager. All the punters I knew up to then were novices, even the ones that had been betting for a while. He was the first guy I had met who studied form beyond the basic daily paper provision.

Q Would it be fair to say he moved you up a level?

Yes, not to the point where I was making it pay but certainly he greatly added to my education.

Q How did things develop from there?

During this spell I began to keep records for the first time and although my maximum bet would be around £50 I seemed to be averaging a £50 profit per week. I perhaps naively thought that all I needed to do was bet £100 and I would double my profit. Of course there is more to it than that. For about two years after that I would perhaps be termed as semi-pro in the sense that I was working the early mornings at Smithfield market and in the afternoons I was travelling to the racetrack to carry out my betting. You have to remember back then you had to go to the course or pay the full betting tax off-course. I did this for about eighteen months but the strain was beginning to tell.

**Q So how did you go about taking the plunge
to full-time punting?**

I was in Chesterfield with some friends enjoying a drink when we
got round to discussing the ideal job we craved. When it came to
my turn I simply said 'professional gambler.' One of the guys asked
why I simply don't go ahead and try. My answer was that I had the
confidence but not the bankroll. He suggested that I get a loan.
On the way back from Chesterfield my wife and I had an in-depth
discussion about the whole idea. There was a lot to consider; the
responsibilities of family life and giving up a steady income were
pretty high on the list. On our return we took out a bank loan,
supposedly for a new kitchen, and armed with my bankroll I set
about my new full-time job as a pro-gambler.

Q How did your wife feel about this arrangement?

She has never questioned or interfered, she lets me get on with it and
I must admit there have been some rough times particularly early on
when I first started. Funnily enough a few years after my start I got
a jackpot up at Royal Ascot and yes, you've guessed it, we bought a
new kitchen so what goes around kind of comes around. I have been
lucky, back then there would have been fifteen or twenty faces you
would regularly see at the tracks. It's not like today with no tax and
Betfair to keep you at home. From what I saw back then I would not
conclude that full-time betting and happily married life went hand
in hand. I have always been very grateful for that support I had back
then, and still enjoy now.

**Q So how did the first few years go armed with
your new bankroll?**

It was a massive learning curve. The very first week coincided with the
start of the jumps season. I was doing some of the southern tracks

and during that first week I won just under 4.5k. But looking back I wish that had not happened because I did think 'hey this is quite easy'. Even the first six months was quite good but I was finding it hard to put the time in to study when coupled with the travelling needed to get to the tracks. I had a good two years before hitting a major blip. It's the losing runs that are the true test of whether you are cut out for professional betting. At one point I questioned how I would work my way out of the downturn. You have to stick to the principles that have served you well in the past and take a disciplined, long-term approach. Around this time a high-profile big punter and owner asked me to share my work with him. He paid a retainer with bonuses. It was a good arrangement and gave me the first taste of how I could share my work with others.

Q Did the arrangement last long?

Overall we had a good few years together before I took my work to a wider audience.

Q What about the blip, what happened there: bad results, bad money management?

Looking back a bit of both really. It's the nature of the business that things will turn against you from time to time. It was that blip, as you call it that taught me the importance of discipline and patience. My staking has not really changed over the years. I would bet horses that I felt were overpriced. If I had a horse at 3-1 and it was available at 6-1 I would bet it as a 3-1 shot. My prices were more accurate than most and this has always been my edge.

Q You have moved forward quickly from novice punter to more advanced topics like race tissues. Who or what promoted these more advanced ways of betting?

I have to go back to my friend from the betting shop. He was formulating tissues and introduced me to the concept. Previously I had never heard of them. I didn't even know what a 100% book was. At first I found it very difficult. Where do you start? Do you start at the top or the bottom and where do you draw your line? A big help was Eddie Fremantle who I would often go racing with. He was pricing up races and I gathered a lot of insight through him.

Q What can you tell us about how you tackle the process of forming a tissue?

I first try and reduce the runners to contenders and those that are non-contenders. After that it's down to form study and looking at how the race will be run, the conditions and who it will suit and then allocating prices based on this. There are no hard rules to it and I am thankful for that otherwise everyone would come up with the same odds. There is some intuition involved but with practice it gets easier. I would do my tissue for the track I was visiting and then back those that were overpriced.

Q Would that be any price above your tissue?

No it would depend on the over-round at the track, some tracks and races were more generous than others. I would often be asked by punters what I fancied, which of course to them means what's going to win. I usually could not answer or at best I would say I am backing this because it's 4-1 and I think it should be 5-2. What has changed in recent years with Betfair is that when a horse looks to be too big a price now, there may be a reason that isn't general knowledge. I do take this into consideration.

Q **Is this a gut feeling or do you have some sort evidence based on data?**

It's based on my own observations and one or two fellow pro punters who I talk to. If we all generally agree on a price and it's twice that on the exchanges, then the alarm bells start ringing. Of course you have to treat each race individually. For example, if *Timeform* have it down as a rogue then that may explain it.

Q **Do you stay away from price forecasts before working on your tissues?**

Yes, I prefer to work in the morning and I ignore betting forecasts.

Q **What about tissue ingredients?**

You have to try and find angles into your analysis that are different from the rest if you are to have an edge. With me I compile my own handicap ratings and these days I feel it is these that give me my edge over the majority of people following the likes of *Timeform*.

Q **If you are no longer full-time on track when are you placing your bets?**

It's difficult to get a bet on with bookmakers in the morning. Early liquidity is also weak on the exchanges, unless it's a strong meeting. Often it's a case of having to wait until the pre-race shows.

Q **What tools do you use as part of your race analysis?**

I use Raceform Interactive to store all my ratings. I also do my own race comments in addition to theirs. I find this very useful because if I read my own comments it triggers the race in my head whereas a *Raceform* or *Timeform* comment doesn't. I also spend a good amount of time studying race recordings to get an insight into a race.

**Q Given the freely available internet race recordings
do you think this area has become more difficult?**

Yes it has and of course there are more people doing it for different
reasons; perhaps to see what horses they can trade in-running rather
than simply back. In the past it used to be an enormous edge simply
being at the races because you would see things that no one else had.
That particular edge has now gone. I come back to my own ratings
and my own comments; they are two of the factors that give me my
edge these days. Having said that I am finding that more races are
corresponding on Betfair to my tissue and this has meant I now have
to prepare more races in order to find an opportunity. I used to be
able to price up six races and then find I could play in two or three
of them. Today I can find myself doing up to twenty races and still
not finding a bet. You have to be prepared to put in the hours, but
remain patient and wait for the right opportunity. I still believe that
selectivity is the key and always the value has to be there.

**Q So are you having fewer bets than you were
say ten years ago?**

Yes, although you do tend to find other ways of making a few quid,
like playing horses that you know are going to be shorter perhaps
in-running.

**Q What about accepting lower margins but cranking up
the action to compensate for the lower ROI%?**

It's required a shift in thinking, I am an out-and-out punter at heart
and backing horses is what I want to do but I am used to a certain
degree of value and backing at less value takes some getting used
to. Even when I back a horse and then lay it in-running at shorter
it bothers me that I am giving value away on the lay to someone at

the track who has quicker access to what is happening. I think it's the value view of betting that's now ingrained in me that gives me that concern. The bottom line is that I am not prepared to bet if the selection is under what I consider to be its true price. However when you do identify an opportunity, you need to try to maximize your returns. Increasing turnover at the wrong times does not fit with my long-term approach.

Q Should this worry you if after all your end of the transaction is working out, maybe without the on-course thieves you would be less likely to get matched?

No I am not sure that's true. If we were all betting in-running from a level playing field I think we would still get matched. There would probably be more in-running players; it would come down to the judgment and knowledge of the players. As it stands at the moment, it doesn't matter how good a judge you are – you cannot give on-course layers four-six seconds' start.

Q What prompted you to launch a tipping line?

I had been full time for a few years when a chap approached me at Haydock and asked if I had ever thought of putting up my bets. I really didn't know what he had in mind. It was the early days of premium rate telephone lines and he gave me a number to call so I could listen to some of the tipsters they had under their management. I wasn't too impressed with what I heard and knew I could provide something better based on my experience of actually betting for a living.

Soon it became apparent to me that I would be happier providing a truly professional service that genuinely reflected my own betting, rather than just mindless daily tipping. I had often been asked on course if I could provide this type of professional service but the extra time needed and the logistics involved just seemed to be against it. I wanted a select group of subscribers ready to take the longer-term approach and I wanted to be confident that I could provide a very high level of customer service. With this in mind I teamed up with a company who look after all my administration and marketing plus we have a dedicated office that handles telephone calls. There is a great deal of backroom horseracing and general betting knowledge that goes into providing the members with a good all-round service. Because I can rely on the backroom staff, I am free to concentrate on my betting. I am not remote as I do speak to members fairly regularly. In the last few weeks I have had telephone conversations with members to give advice on handicapping and buying a racehorse.

Q What about the old chestnut, why a tipping line if you can make it pay yourself?

Obviously it's a business like many others. I am selling my knowledge and expertise. However, it goes further than that. This is not a "get rich quick" scheme, we have been providing a service founded upon honesty and integrity for the best part of fifteen years. I get a great deal of satisfaction from members who have sent thanks over the years for helping them to bet more professionally.

Q One word that's bound to create a lively debate is value, do you think the media really understand the word?

Most people do not understand value, they think it simply means big prices whereas to me a 20-1 shot is no value if it should be 33-1. I think it's quite a high-level skill being able to recognize value even when you understand what it means. Many of the channels will simply employ some ex-jockey who will proceed to tell the public that he has had a word with this or that trainer and that's often the sum total of their preparation. The result of this is that the viewing public never get beyond the 'he is riding for this trainer so that's the one I want to be with' kind of thinking. In fact if you sit down and talk them through the reasons a horse should be a price the majority are not interested, they would rather hear about the whispers and the price is irrelevant; thankfully there are still people betting like this on the exchanges. For me information does have its value, but only when it is applied with detailed knowledge of the form.

Q We have mentioned the exchanges, what other changes have you noticed?

National Hunt handicapping seems to have changed quite a bit. So many loopholes have been plugged that I am convinced many trainers have to run more horses under their merit to get them handicapped than they used to do. The bigger stables often have so much in hand with many of their horses that it does not seem to affect them as much. It may be a cynical view but I also think the exchanges provide the platform for making a few quid whilst getting your horse handicapped. It's always happened but not to the extent that it happens nowadays. What this means is where before the exchanges I was purely price orientated, I do these days take into account the exchanges. Of course it's not always alarm bells, today there was a novice chase where the difference in price between the favourite and second favourite was just too great; the disparity was easy to account for because everyone had tipped up the favourite who had been greatly hyped up. To reiterate; you have to treat each race on its own merits.

Q Finally what advice would you give to any aspiring pro punter?

I know what I would have said eight years ago: Be completely knowledgeable, throw yourself into it. I work over one hundred hours a week during the peak months and know that if you don't put the hours in, you will miss good opportunities. You need to prove yourself profitable to smaller stakes and then gradually increase and of course remember it is all about the price and value. These days I think it's slightly changed. There are far more areas to get involved in and of course more sports. But to answer your question – everything revolves around value; that's all that matters.

INTERVIEWED IN APRIL 2011

Chapter 10

JON BABB

The interviewing of Jon Babb for the book started out as something of a gut feeling. I had no prior knowledge of Jon's betting achievements when he came across my radar. In fact I had never heard of him on the day I heard him speak as a co-presenter on William Hill radio. Pretty much all the radio and TV pundits are selection driven rather than value driven. In other words they are hoping to bag one or two winners on the afternoon to avoid looking stupid, in the knowledge that the next time they appear a clean slate will be waiting and the whole process can begin again. There is little or no accountability and no interest in long-term profit. Jon's chat, however, was entirely different; he clearly spoke on air in a manner that would not be amiss if we put all the contributors to this book in a room together and asked them to review the afternoon's racing. After hearing him a few times I was convinced that he knew the time of day when it came to profitable betting. We met up at Wolverhampton racecourse where he was doing the paddock profiling for the radio station. Conspiracy theorists note, William Hill radio appear to have moved him into this role. We had a long and enjoyable chat in the restaurant of the on-course Holiday Inn and my initial views of Jon were confirmed.

Q How did you first get interested in racing and betting?

Initially through my father and his father who were interested in racing. I always remember Saturdays going to watch Wolves or going racing, it was one or the other. I don't remember preferring one over the other but the fascination with betting and the money soon took over. I first started betting when I was about nine or ten, just a small amount to have a bet with. Although it was a small amount and it was given to me I still wanted to win, the winning was important even from a very early age.

Q Was that attitude to winning something you got from your father?

No not really, my father wanted to win and he took it seriously with the weekly Handicap Book but he was happy if he broke even and had a good day out. To be fair he had a job to hold down but from very early on I saw that you could win at the game. My first attempt at professional punting was in 1983 at the age of twenty. I survived for four years but back then there were a lot of things against you, mainly betting tax and the fact that the margins were bigger, and I could not really get going and was unable to put together a substantial pot. With the need to buy a house looming I decided to go back into regular work.

Q Did it not work with your first attempt due to lack of initial bank or was it your betting method?

Probably a bit of both really, I started off with a couple of grand but buying a house was the problem. To get a mortgage you needed a job with a "regular" income. I decided therefore to go back to work and rethink where I was going. From 1986 to the late 1990s I had a job in financial services and my betting became part time. I was good at sales and earned good money in financial services but most importantly I could often be finished by around 1pm leaving the afternoons free for racing. I would be working from about 6am to 8.30am on the day's races before going to work. In the afternoons I was racing every day with a close friend.

Q Tell me a little about the friend.

I had known him a long time, he was a successful punter and by this time he had his own office with SIS which outside of bookmakers was pretty much unheard of then. We went back a long way from a betting shop in Wolverhampton. It was invaluable being able to tap into his resources and also see how he worked as he had never stopped, whereas I had taken a few years out. During this period I decided that I would not go full time again until I had a substantial pot, one which could sustain me through those poor periods.

Q Where were you betting during this period and were there problems getting on?

Mainly with phone accounts, I was not betting in huge amounts. In the 90s there was a golden period when bookmakers seemed to want to take your money. You seemed to be able to get anything on. Even when the exchanges started the bookmakers seemed to take very little notice of them. It was as if they were growing in the background and it was only a couple of years into their emergence that they realized that the monster was there to bite them. I think they thought that it was simply going to go away and to some extent they were caught with their pants down.

Q What was the next stage in your punting arrangements and what prompted this change?

The pressure of holding down a full-time job with a large company and punting pretty much full time was getting to me. I was putting in a lot of hours and although I did not become ill from it I sensed at one stage that if I continued with my schedule I would become ill. At this stage I had enough money and of course things were changing in the late 90s. Spread betting was coming through and I won a lot of money on the spreads. The margins the firms were working to on spread betting back then seemed smaller and this was obviously helpful, along with the fact that their pricing was awful. I used to get a cheque from Sporting, City or IG Index nearly every week and they did not seem to mind. The lady cashier at my bank seemed to think I worked for them.

Q So you felt around 1999 that you needed to change things, what did you do?

I packed in with the financial service work. I had been making money betting on the side and this money was always on top of what I needed so it was easy to save quite a bit of money. Betting for a living was always what I wanted to do. I wanted to escape the nine to five and given that I would not consider myself an entrepreneur, betting was a way out. Having said that the security thinking kicked in again and I bought a local bookmakers, although not with the intention of working in it. I would not have contemplated it if I did not have a good manager available to run it. My commitment was to cover days off and holidays etc, but little more than that on a day-to-day basis.

Q **Was this a good move given that exchanges were about to explode?**

It wasn't a bad move but selling it at the price I sold it for probably was. I probably let it go a little on the cheap side especially as I might have seen the coming potential of FOBTs. The truth is I was moving house and did not fancy the extra commuting distance to get into the shop even on a casual basis. I did not have the shop for that long and it's fair to say I probably could have got a bit more for it but financially it was not my primary concern at the time. I probably failed to factor in the FOBT potential of the business when negotiating the sale price.

Q **So you now moved solely into betting as a means of income, did you not also get involved in racehorse ownership?**

Yes, I first got involved with some friends after a trainer asked me to help with form analysis. Once involved with horse ownership I became more interested in some aspects of training horses such as placing them, getting them handicapped and even the purchasing side. I found getting to know a little about this side of the industry helped with betting.

Q **Anything else help you along with the betting skills?**

One thing I used to do from a very early stage was study past results. I would not just go home after a day's racing and think about the next day, I would look at the day's results and see if I could figure out why I might have backed this winner or that winner. I would also look at the winner's past races and see how it arrived at the win. Sometimes it would be obvious if it was going for its fourth win on the trot but sometimes other, more subtle reasons could be found. It was this activity that brought my attention to the draw and got me marking up draw biases. Also the pace of the race, which came later but nevertheless had an influence on how I would view a race. When I started out in racing they would simply be stalls one to eight, I did not attach any importance to where they were coming from or how the pace of the race would be formed. Reviewing past races in this way was a good way to bring new angles to my attention. I would often hear people saying "how could you pick that out?" after a 20-1 shot had gone in. For me these were the ones I wanted to back, I was not interested in the short-priced horses. In fact it was one of my betting agents who pointed out that although I was profitable overall it was away from the front of the market where I became more profitable.

Q What about staking, how do you approach this area?

I don't have a set formula, in other words I don't say it's 5-1 so I will have x pounds on. I rely more on gut instinct which I think I have developed over the years. I do of course have a range of bet sizes that I work within but there is no strict formula that I use for each bet. One thing I have learnt is that the small "action" bet is probably something everyone would benefit from leaving out. If you are having a small bet then it's probably not worth having. I think you have to notice the difference to focus the thinking. My staking has just gradually grown over the years as my pot has grown. I probably would not have believed 20 years ago that I would have a thousand pounds on a horse, but it's down to confidence and the bank growing behind you.

Q What things or people were pivotal in moving your betting forward?

Seeing real people around me that could make it pay. The chap I knew from the 1980s who I met in my local bookmakers could make it pay and for me it was important to see tangible evidence of someone making it pay rather than simply reading about it. Keep it simple is always good advice, whether it be speed figures, sectional times or anything else. I always thought that I started ten years too late. If I had started ten years earlier I would be sat in Barbados now. I can see me reaching a point maybe in five or ten years when I will not want to do this any more on a daily basis.

Q Do you use speed figures or sectional times, and if so whose?

I think the *Racing Post*'s Topspeed are as good as any and combining those with collateral ratings is a good starting point. I try not to look at too many otherwise you can over-complicate things and end up never having a bet. I prefer sectionals over the jumps as it's easier to log them and on the Flat you only have to be slightly out for it to be quite significant. Some tracks on the Flat are quite impossible, the Newbury straight course for example has little in the way of reference points on which to clock times. I have looked at and respect Racing Research and RSB ratings but was put off Racing Research ratings by the layout and by RSB because there is no indication of what they consist of. I like to have some idea of how ratings are compiled and I like to apply them myself and decide what is value whereas RSB tended to tell you what is value. What I prefer to do is first of all mark off the races that I know I will be interested in at the 48-hour declaration stage. For example the 20-runner sprint races will get thrown out straight away. This mean the next morning I have the races I want to go through ready.

Q How do you know which races to select?

It's a feel really for the shape of a race. I like each-way races so 15-runner handicaps will go out. That does not mean I will not look at these races later from a different perspective, for example I may find something I want to lay or place lay in one of the non-bet races. I have a few clients but I do not put out lays to them as I feel that laying requires a different mindset and it is not suited to everyone. There are certain tracks I do not bet at, for example Brighton and Folkestone so any races there will go out.

Q Why do you omit certain tracks?

I just don't think the form holds up from those tracks so I don't scrutinize them and I think many horses simply don't handle those tracks. I am very dubious of seaside tracks generally although to a lesser extent at Yarmouth. Tomorrow for example I like Thirsk, which has always been a profitable track for me. I will be looking at all the maidens along with eight-to-ten-runner handicaps. I am not too keen on two-mile races. I think the pace in them can be dubious and you are generally dealing with slow horses. I will do twelve-furlong races but I know some good judges who won't go beyond ten furlongs. Although I am ordinarily not a great fan of sprint handicaps, I like it when you feel you can split a race in two when you really feel there is a strong track advantage more than is already priced in to the market. This can often be the case in six-furlong handicaps and I particularly like it if you can get sixteen-plus runners. When you can split the field you can then really concentrate on the each-way factor.

Q Would the draw be the factor here?

Usually. I can remember when Southwell used to have 16-runner handicaps and you could virtually guarantee four horses to finish at least in the first six. You could simply back four horses each-way and make a profit. Today they would bet 11-4, 7-2, 9-2 whereas back in those days they would chalk up 4-1, 5-1, 6-1. The forecasts used to be good value as well but they are more clued up now.

Q What other factors come into the mix when making your selections?

The collateral ratings come into it, that is to say what's met what and how have they fared against each other? I like *Timeform Perspective* and of course the speed ratings I have already told you about. Also trainer form, although I prefer smaller trainers to the bigger trainers where things can get a bit woolly. Richard Hannon for example has two yards so you would have to split his runners to realistically analyze them. I prefer to scrutinize small yards particularly if they have runners not necessarily winning but outperforming their odds. So I may see a smallish trainer having a 33-1 shot finish fourth followed the next day by a 20-1 shot finishing fifth. I then keep an eye on this trainer as he may be ready to hit form. If you wait until his winning figures are in the paper for this kind of trainer, it's too late. You have to anticipate their run into form.

Q You mentioned earlier to me "the grind" surrounding the job. Is this the analysis or the execution of the betting?

Both really, it starts early morning with the preparation for the day's betting and then quickly runs into the afternoon's betting activity. You have to try and fit a break in late morning even if it is only to go out and get some fresh air. Of course night racing begins next week and the whole thing can then run right into the night. Occasionally I am tempted to put off reviewing past races until the next day but I find things work best if I review a day's racing on the same day when events are fresh in my mind. I always take a holiday after Royal Ascot but even that creates a catching-up period when I return, although I tend to ease in during this period and kind of wait until my back form is in full swing again. To be honest I don't back many horses that have not run for a couple of months anyway.

Q Is that quite a strong parameter for you?

I would rather not back a horse that had not run for a longer period than six to eight weeks. I appreciate that for higher-class horses breaks of six weeks may be dictated by their opportunities but lower-grade horses, especially geldings, should be able to run within 40 days. If they have not then I just get a bit cautious about them to be honest. I would rather take one that had been off for 150 days as they are more likely to be hard trained for that particular day. The trouble with 40- or 50-day horses is you don't quite know what the problem has been.

Q Do you have any rules regarding race grade, for example will you not bet below a certain race grade?

Quite the opposite, I would be more of a class four, five, six player than a class one. I find there are more pricing errors in these races. How many pricing errors will you find in the Derby or the National? They have been betting on it since last year's race. It is a bit like lower league football, there are probably more errors in the conference than the premier league. The horses in the higher grade are so well known and this is factored into their prices. On Saturday most people will be focusing on the Grand National meeting and possibly one or two other cards. The fourth or fifth meeting on the day will be overlooked and with little liquidity on Betfair, bookmakers will be pricing up on fragile markets. I have confidence in what I do and the fact that I can exploit this. Most people are excited about backing a winner at Aintree, I don't care where I back a winner.

Q You create your own tissue, tell me a bit about that process.

I don't do every race, only those I have highlighted as the kind of race that would interest me. First of all I do not look at any price forecasts or tipsters as this might influence me. What might surprise you is the fact that I tend to do it differently to everyone else. I do all the outsiders first and then move on to the rest of the field. For example in a ten-runner handicap I might identify the race as five and five, that is to say five horses I think can win and five I don't like. The five I don't like I might view from the point of view of what price would I want to throw a fiver at them. This gives me a starting point from which to price them up. When I have done the outsiders I will take a look at what percentage I have got left. Doing it this way I feel I tend to get the favourite the right price more often than not. I suspect that if I start with the favourite I am more likely to get the favourite wrongly priced although I am not quite sure why that would be. I feel it is important to get the prices right on the fancied five as it is in this area that I will be betting.

Q Any advice on losing runs and how to cope with them?

I would not stop betting because you can never tell when your form is going to return. I would not put people off scaling back a little with bet size when you feel out of form. Find a period of time for reflection other than immediately after a losing race and look through your bets and ask yourself whether you have been betting any different. Hopefully you should say no, and if that's the case carry on regardless.

Q What initial basic advice would you give to a losing punter who has aspirations of becoming profitable?

Many punters have too many bets so I would say log your bets and analyze them and strip out the bad bets. I have already mentioned that I don't bet at Brighton as in the past I noticed that I was losing money there. Clearly me and Brighton don't get on so I don't bet there. Once you have identified in what areas you are profitable you can scale up your betting there. Too many punters don't have to bet to eat and as such they bet on anything and everything. You have to be ahead of the other punters. For example you might spot a draw bias early in the day on Great St Wilfrid day at Ripon. This means you have to be armed to react quickly to any value prices later on the card as you won't be the only person spotting it. People were half asleep ten or fifteen years ago but these days it is more competitive.

INTERVIEWED IN MAY 2011

INDEX